GOD'S BLUEPRINT FOR A HAPPY, HEALTHY, ENDURING MARRIAGE

TYLER SCOTT

ISBN

THE MARRIAGE REF © 2011 by Tyler Scott
All rights reserved.

ISBN PRINT: 978-0-9849618-3-2
ISBN eBOOK: 978-0-9849618-4-9

All Scripture quotations, unless otherwise indicated, are taken from the Holy Bible, New International Version®, NIV® Copyright © 1973, 1978, 1984, 2010 by Biblica, Inc.™ Used by permission. All rights reserved worldwide.

Cover Design by: Josh May Media | joshmaymedia.com
Interior Book Design by Sarah O'Neal | eve custom artwork

To order this book, please visit www.condeopress.com

To Bridget.
I love you.
Always have.
You're my favorite in the whole wide world.

CONTENTS

Acknowledgements
Introduction: *Who Is the Marriage Ref?*
1 | Forget The Scoreboard
2 | The Marriage Ref
3 | The Marriage Covenant
4 | Covenant Relationship—or Consumer Relationship?
5 | "Love *ME!*"
6 | Naked and Unashamed
7 | From Selfishness to Servanthood
8 | Hear the Call
9 | Understand the Fall
10 | Hold the Ball
11 | Win the Crowd!
12 | Who is Your Crowd?
13 | Living Out Loud
Epilogue: *Do You Need a Miracle?*
Notes
A Word to Victims of Abuse

ACKNOWLEDGMENTS

Thank you:

to Jesus for your grace, and for calling me to serve my bride and your bride, in that order.

to Bridget for being a loving wife, an amazing mom to our boys, and modeling a Christ-like attitude and approach to life. Simply put: you love God, and you love others. You are my best friend, and the most attractive person I know.

to Trevor, Owen and Cole for loving your Daddy unconditionally. Watching you laugh, play and grow is the purest joy I know. *Delight yourself in the Lord, and He will give you the desires of your heart* (Psalm 37:4). The mere thought that this book could help you love and serve your future wives brings tears to my eyes.

to Mom and Jim, Dad and France, Amanda, and Nona for your love, perseverance, guidance, generosity, friendship and support. I love you, and thank God often for each of you.

to my Neighborhood Church family for trusting me to write this book on God's blueprint for marriage, and for the opportunity to serve God's people on an exceptional Leadership Team (with Larry, Jim, Mark and Danny) and Staff. It is a privilege to experience life transformation through following Christ together, and to contend for the Gospel alongside great friends.

to Bert and Dru, Ben and Kelly, Tom and Karen, Kevin and Sasha, Len and Michael, Chris and Heather, and Tim and Courtney for your faithful partnership in this project. I am humbled by your friendship and support. Bert– special thanks to you for pushing me (for years) to write a book for one simple reason: to influence people for the Gospel.

to Phil for your abiding friendship of 25 years. This section would be incomplete without acknowledging you. Any time spent with you and Sabrina is a gift for which Bridget and I are grateful.

to Jim Denney, for using your God-given talents to help me produce and prepare this manuscript for print. Let's do this again sometime.

INTRODUCTION

Who is the Marriage Ref?

This book began as a series of talks at the Neighborhood Church of Castro Valley, California, in the fall of 2010. The morning I was to give the first talk in the series, a couple stopped me in the lobby and said, "Tyler, I heard you were going to talk about 'The Marriage Ref,' and we thought you'd show up in a referee's jersey."

Well, I had actually considered showing up in my striped ref's jersey, but I realized that to do so would give the wrong impression. Like I said, I'm not the Marriage Ref. I don't have a rulebook in one hand and a whistle in the other. I can't stand on the sidelines of your marriage and enforce the rules. Even if I could, I don't have the authority to make you or your spouse do what I say.

So who is the Marriage Ref? He's the One who designed the marriage covenant, the One who wrote the rules, the One who has all authority over our lives. It's the One who has the knowledge and wisdom to tell us how the marriage relationship should work.

As followers of Christ, we believe that the Designer and Initiator of marriage is God the Creator. He wrote the rules, and He's the authority on how a marriage is supposed to function. God is the Marriage Ref. If we want to have a healthy and happy marriage, we need to follow His rules and His advice.

When you bought your car, you probably didn't stop to think about it, but there was a vast team of men and women who designed every component of that car, from the engine and transmission to the cup-holders and the CD player. Open the glove compartment and you'll find an owner's manual written by the people who designed the car. The manual tells you everything about how to use that vehicle, from the maintenance of the engine to the operation of the power windows.

The people who wrote the manual know how your car works and how to maintain it so it will function at peak performance. A wise car owner will study the manual and familiarize himself with its advice. You ignore the wisdom in your owner's manual at your own peril.

The same is true of marriage. There's an owners manual for your marriage, and if you and your marriage partner heed the advice in that manual, you'll have a healthy marriage. Ignore the wisdom in the owner's manual, and you're taking a huge risk.

God is the Marriage Ref. He wrote the manual. He's the One we must heed in order to have a healthy, functional marriage.

1
FORGET THE SCOREBOARD

When I played football in high school, one of my best friends was a defensive lineman named Tony. He was an inch taller and more than a hundred pounds bigger than I was. As a wide receiver, my job was to sprint downfield, catch the ball, and score touchdowns. Because Tony was a defensive lineman, he didn't have a lot of opportunities to score touchdowns. He was always butting heads with the offensive line and trying to take down the opponent's quarterback.

In one game, lo and behold, Tony was on the field and the other team fumbled the ball. Tony snatched up the ball and ran it into the end zone for a touchdown. He went crazy celebrating, because a defensive lineman rarely gets to score a touchdown. After the game, he gave himself a nickname—"Hey, I'm Touchdown Tony!"

Tony's touchdown came early in the season—so early that I had only scored one touchdown, even though I played wide receiver on offense. He really played that up. "Hey, Tyler," he said, "how many touchdowns do you have?" I'd say, "One." "Okay, now ask me." I played along. "Hey, Tony, how many touchdowns do you have?" "One! We're tied!"

Well, the season went along, and we got into the high school playoffs. So there we were in a big playoff game—and Tony got his opportunity again. The opposing team was backed up on their own six yard line. The quarterback took the snap—and fumbled the ball. Again, Touchdown Tony seized the opportunity and scooped up the ball. He was just five yards from the end zone and another unlikely touchdown, but he couldn't see that.

Somehow, in the scrum, Tony got turned around. He opened his eyes, saw 95 yards of green grass, and he took off running—*in the wrong direction*!

It was pandemonium on the football field! All of Tony's teammates chased after him as he crossed the fifty, the forty, the thirty! Our defensive guys were doing their best to catch him and keep him from scoring for the other team. They yelled at him to stop, but Tony didn't even look back.

Finally, three of our guys ganged up on him and dragged him down on the four yard line. Tony jumped and shouted, "What are you doing! I almost had a touchdown!"

In unison, his teammates shouted, "You were going the wrong way!"

Almost two decades later, people still call him Touchdown Tony—not for the touchdown he made early in the season, but for the wrong-way touchdown he nearly scored for the other team. He's remembered not for all the great things he did that season, but for one spectacular mistake.

What does this story have to do with your marriage relationship?

Simply this: If you are a wife, don't turn your husband into "Touchdown Tony." If you are a husband, don't turn your wife into "Touchdown Antonia." Don't focus on the one mistake your marriage partner makes, forgetting all the wonderful things your marriage partner does throughout the year.

If you want to have a strong marriage, a healthy marriage, a marriage that is satisfying and honoring to God, then focus on everything that is true, noble, pure, lovely, admirable, excellent, and praiseworthy about your spouse. Don't remind your spouse of that one mistake. Don't bring it up in front of other people. Above all, don't mention it in front of your kids.

Don't give your spouse a negative reputation, a negative self-image, or a negative nickname like Touchdown Tony.

"Submit to one another"

You want to have a happy marriage, a great marriage, a godly marriage. That's why you're reading this book. Yet I know that some of the people reading these pages are facing a crisis in the marriage. There's pain, there's conflict, there are emotions of sorrow—and anger.

I know that some people reading this book have given up on their marriage. Some are planning an escape route, a separation, a divorce. If that's your situation, then my prayer for you right now is that God would illuminate His Word for you and enable you to persevere and discover the true meaning of married love, the meaning of Christian love. I pray that God would win you and your spouse back to each other and back to Himself. God knows our weakness and He wants to bring us His strength.

In this chapter, we're going to focus on one verse of Scripture. It's a short verse, but it's packed with practical application and personal accountability and profound theological meaning. That verse is Ephesians 5:21: "Submit to one another out of reverence for Christ."

Now, there's a phrase we don't hear very often: "Submit to one another." This is a command to *mutually* submit—and this is the umbrella statement as to how we are to have marriages that are Christ-centered and that reflect the good news of Jesus Christ. This is the central truth of this chapter, so permit me to underscore it:

> *Mutual submission is the key to this verse and the key to a functioning, healthy marriage.*

What does the word "submit" mean? In the original Greek language of the New Testament, it is the word *hupotassó*, meaning to place oneself in subjection to another person. It is a military term that has the original sense of "to arrange oneself under," to arrange one's interests, attitude, and preferences in subjection and submission—for example, to one's superior officer. In the sense in which Paul uses this phrase, he's saying that couples are to arrange their lives in submission to each other.

This is a challenging command—especially in the context of our own self-centered, self-indulgent, me-first North American culture. But the truth is that the entire Gospel message, the good news of Jesus Christ, runs counter to the culture we live in.

In Philippians 2:3, Paul says, "Do nothing out of selfish ambition or vain conceit, but in humility consider others better than yourselves." That is what submission is supposed to look like. The biblical concept of mutual submission is based on *humility*—our deliberate choice to consider the needs and interests of others ahead of our own.

In 1 Corinthians 13, Paul gives us the most famous passage ever written on the subject of love. For this reason, it is often read at weddings:

> If I speak in the tongues of men or of angels, but do not have love, I am only a resounding gong or a clanging cymbal. If I have the gift of prophecy and can fathom all mysteries and all knowledge, and if I have a faith that can move mountains, but do not have love, I am nothing. If I give all I possess to the poor and give over my body to hardship that I may boast, but do not have love, I gain nothing.
>
> Love is patient, love is kind. It does not envy, it does not boast, it is not proud. It does not dishonor others, it is not self-seeking, it is not easily angered, it keeps no record of wrongs. Love does not delight in evil but rejoices with the truth. It always protects, always trusts, always hopes, always perseveres.
>
> Love never fails. But where there are prophecies, they will cease; where there are tongues, they will be stilled; where there is knowledge, it will pass away. For we know in part and we prophesy in part, but when completeness comes, what is in part disappears. When I was a child, I talked like a child, I thought like a child, I reasoned like a child. When I became a man, I put the ways of childhood behind me. For now we see only a reflection as in a mirror; then we shall see face to face. Now I know in part; then I shall know fully, even as I am fully known.
>
> And now these three remain: faith, hope and love. But the greatest of these is love (1 Corinthians 13:1-13).

This passage describes the love God has for you and me. And it describes the love I must have for my wife Bridget, and that you ought to have in your marriage relationship. The special kind of love Paul writes about in 1 Corinthians 13 is not a feeling, not an emotion. It's a decision, an act of the will.

God loves you and me with this kind of amazing love. Do we love others—do I love my wife, do you love your husband or wife—with such a love as this?

The six ways we keep score

If you and I are honest with ourselves, we have to admit that we often fall short of this kind of love in our own lives. Instead of loving one another and mutually submitting to one another, we frequently do the exact opposite. What is the opposite of love and mutual submission? I call it "keeping score."

We all know what a scoreboard is—a large billboard-size panel used to display the scores and statistics at a sporting event. The scoreboard tells you who is winning and who is losing, and by how much. In sports, it's important to know the score. It's human nature to keep score. But in a marriage, keeping score and choosing winners and losers is one of the fastest ways of killing a relationship.

How do we keep score in a marriage? Let me suggest six ways all of us tend to keep score in our marriage relationships.

First, we keep score by keeping *tallies*. The word "tally" means to determine the sum of two or more numbers. In a sports setting, we tally up (that is, we keep a running total) of the points scored by the two teams, so we know who is winning and who is losing. In a marriage we tally up the wrongs that are done to us by our marriage partner. We remember who did what to whom. We remember the harsh word, the thoughtless act, the insult, the argument, the chore that didn't get done, the hurtful words that can never be taken back. We keep a tally, and we check it daily.

Then, when there is *another* thoughtless act or hurtful word, we take out our mental tally sheet, and we mark down another sin. And we say, "You did it again! Now you've *really* done it! I'm *never* going to forget what you did to me!"

It's interesting how everyone's tally comes out lopsided. Our own wrongs are just minor infractions, while the wrongs committed by our mate are flagrant violations!

Second, we keep score with our *tone*. I have a circle of close personal friends who support me and hold me accountable in my walk with Christ. These accountability partners have half-jokingly, half-seriously dubbed themselves the Tone Police. They hold me accountable for my tone of voice. They tell me, "Tyler, sometimes you have a tough time with your tone, and especially with the way you talk to Bridget."

They like to imitate the way I say Bridget's name when I get a bit exasperated. They have heard me say Bridget's name in such a way that it is truly the ultimate in keeping score. There's no way to accurately reproduce my tone with words on paper, but it comes out something like "*BRIDG-ET!*"

If she happens to do something I don't agree with it, I say, "*BRIDG-ET!*" And if the Tone Police overhear me, I can count on them echoing "*BRIDG-ET!*" in that same tone. They're joking, but they make a serious point—and I stand convicted of keeping score through my tone of voice.

Third, we keep score with a game called *tit-for-tat*. We say, "Oh, you did *that*? Well, I'm going to do *this*!" A wife may say, "You went to lunch with the guys? Fine! I'm going to get a mani-pedi!" Or, "You took off an hour early from work? Fine! I'm going out for coffee, the kids are all yours."

And we guys can play this game, too. We say, "Oh, you just bought a new blouse? Okay, I just bought a *boat*! How do you like that?" It's another way we keep score, and it's destructive to the marriage and to Christlike love.

Fourth, we keep score with *facial tics*. We use subtle expressions of disapproval. A small frown. A roll of the eyes. A lift of the brow.

Once in our household, I made a remark that Bridget disapproved of. She took me aside and whispered, "Don't say that in front of our children! You know what little imitators they are!"

"But I didn't say it in front of the boys!"

"They were in earshot. I'm sure they heard every word."

"No they didn't!"

Well, a short time later, we all gathered around the dinner table and gave thanks for the food. Then Trevor, our oldest, spoke up—

And he used *the very same phrase* I had used—the phrase I was so sure he couldn't have heard.

For a husband, the second-worst feeling in the world is when he's proven wrong and his wife is proven right. What's the worst? When his wife gives him that little facial tic that says, "I told you so!"

The instant Trevor said that phrase, Bridget gave me *that* look—that little raised eyebrow, almost imperceptible—but to me it was as loud as a shout. She didn't say a word. She didn't need to. But she was keeping score— "That's minus one point for you, Tyler, and plus one for me."

(And yes, Bridget gave me permission to use this story.)

We all do this. We all find ways to get our message across, with or without words.

Fifth, we keep score with *taunting*. A typical marital taunt goes like this: "I *told* you so, but you wouldn't listen. You just *had* to go and do it your own way! You *never* do what I ask you to do! You *always* do such-and-such!"

You've heard phrases like those—and you've probably said them a time or two. Maybe seeing those words in print makes you wince. Nobody likes to be told they messed up. Most of us respond better to kindness and understanding than we do to taunting, to verbal beat-downs like "you always" and "you never."

Taunting is a serious infraction. In football, a taunting penalty is fifteen yards, the same penalty you get for roughing the passer or spearing a player with your helmet. In marriage, taunting is even more serious, because it is corrosive to the relationship. Outwardly, it builds tension within the marriage. Inwardly, it undermines trust and intimacy. And overall, it's just another way of keeping score.

Sixth, we keep score by *telling others*. This is probably the most destructive form of keeping score. There are few actions more hurtful than taking a private issue and making it public.

A husband goes out with the guys, still angry because of the fight he had with his wife. "You'll never believe what my wife did last night! Let me tell you about this ball and chain I married!" Or a wife goes out with her girlfriends and says, "My husband is such an idiot! Let me tell you the latest!" Have you ever witnessed this kind of behavior? Have you ever engaged in it? Have you ever shared intimate details of your marriage relationship that would hurt or embarrass your spouse?

That kind of behavior is one of the most destructive forms of keeping score. The marriage covenant should serve as a boundary, a zone of protection around the marriage—and when we tell others something negative about our marriage partner, we violate that boundary and remove that protection. We bring enormous harm to the one person we've vowed to love, serve, and protect.

Remember the story of Touchdown Tony. A person can do all the right things, day after day after day, then make one big mistake—and that mistake becomes a reputation for life. Don't do that to your husband. Don't do that to your wife. Don't give the one you love a bad reputation to live down. Give your spouse a great reputation to live up to. Always bless your husband or your wife with your words—never curse.

Above all, remember the biblical definition of love. The apostle Paul tells us that love is patient and kind, love never dishonors or ridicules others, it always protects, and it keeps no record of wrongs. In short, love does not keep score.

Forget the scoreboard

Tallies, tone, tit-for-tat, facial tics, taunting, and telling others—these are the six ways we keep score in the marriage relationship. I have to be honest. When I look at that list, I realize I'm six for six. I've committed every one of those sins, most of them in just the past week. And in so doing, I have sabotaged my own marriage covenant! I often fall short of the biblical standard for a godly husband.

But I won't settle for being the kind of husband I've always been. I'm committed to continual growth in my character, in my faith, in obedience to God's word, and in demonstrating true Christlike love for my wife Bridget. And because of that commitment, I want to dismantle the scoreboard in our marriage. I'm determined to forget the scoreboard, erase it, blot it out with spray paint, obliterate it. I invite you to join me in that commitment—to stop keeping score.

Remember Paul's command in Ephesians 5:21: "Submit to one another out of reverence for Christ." Submit to one another by forgetting the scoreboard. Submit to one another by forgiving and loving and protecting one another.

Now, why should we do that? If your spouse treats you unfairly or criticizes you, if you are feeling angry and hurt, why should you submit to him or her? Why should you protect your marriage partner's reputation? Why shouldn't you engage in a little taunting, a little tit-for-tat? Why should you forgive?

There's one simple answer to all of those questions: Because that's what Jesus did for you. He erased your scoreboard and forgave you, even while you were in rebellion against Him. As God tells us in the Old Testament:

> "I, even I, am he who blots out
>   your transgressions, for my own sake,
>   and remembers your sins no more" (Isaiah 43:25).

In other words, God says to you and me, "I have forgotten your scoreboard."

God's forgiveness toward us is not for our benefit alone. He has forgiven us so that we would go out and become examples to others of the power of His forgiveness. As the apostle Peter wrote, "'He himself bore our sins' in his body on the cross, so that we might die to sins *and live for righteousness*; 'by his wounds you have been healed'" (1 Peter 2:24, emphasis added).

And Paul, earlier in Ephesians, wrote that our forgiveness toward one another is a grateful response to God's forgiveness toward us. He writes, "Be kind and compassionate to one another, forgiving each other, just as in Christ God forgave you" (Ephesians 4:32).

How do we live out these biblical principles of mutual submission and mutual forgiveness in the rough-and-tumble, day-to-day struggles that are common to every marriage? The answer is easy to state, though not always easy to do: Believe the best in your spouse—never assume the worst. Give your partner the benefit of the doubt. Trust that the one who married you is for you, not against you, in his or her heart.

Sometimes your marriage partner will do things that seem hard to understand, inexplicable, or irrational. Sometimes he or she will seem to act out of character. When your marriage partner's behavior is baffling, don't be too quick to judge. Don't be too quick to attach negative motivations to troubling behavior. Pray for your spouse, and ask God to give you patience, sensitivity, and empathy. Talk to your spouse and try to understand his or her problems and motivations. Be a good listener. Build bridges of understanding, not walls of hostility and judgment.

All of this—being quick to forgive, quick to listen, quick to believe the best, and slow to judge—is part of what it means to mutually submit to one another. And it is all part of what it means to forget the scoreboard.

Choose to believe the best

So what does it *really* look like to stop keeping score and truly believe the best about your spouse? It's not a once-for-all thing. It's a series of continual choices you make in order to have a happy marriage.

One of my favorite things to do is leave work at my church office a little early and surprise Bridget and the boys by getting home ahead of schedule. I *love* spending time—quality time, quantity time, any kind of time!—with my family. I'm sure you can relate. But what about those times when your spouse gets home *later* than promised? And later than your expectations? One of the most common sources of conflict in a marriage is that gap between your expectations and your spouse's behavior.

How should we respond when there is a gap between expectation and behavior? What happens when I promise to be home at 5 p.m., and I get held up meeting with a couple at church, and then I don't get home until 6 p.m.? Now there is a one-hour gap between Bridget's expectation and my behavior. How will Bridget respond?

When Bridget gets back from her work later than I expect, how will I respond? When she doesn't fold the laundry how I fold the laundry, how will I respond? When I don't stock the refrigerator like she would stock the refrigerator, how will she respond? When I don't watch the kids the same way she watches the kids (for example, when I watch more sports on TV than she would), how will she respond?

You get the idea. And here's the application: When there's a gap between your expectation and your spouse's behavior, it's important to *choose to believe the best* about your spouse. Over and over again, you have to make that choice in order to stay in love and maintain a happier, healthier marriage. You have to trust that your spouse is a good-willed man or woman. Your spouse is *for* you, *for* your family, *for* your kids.

Bridget needs to choose to believe that I *wanted* to be home early every night, that I *wanted* to spend as much time at home withy my family as I could. But something came up, something I couldn't help, something I regretted as much as Bridget did. So I couldn't keep my promise, I couldn't meet that expectation.

And when Bridget doesn't meet my expectations, I have to choose to believe the best of her. I have to choose to believe that she loves to do the laundry for our family, but sometimes she doesn't have time to fold it perfectly. She has to choose to believe that even though I watch more sports with the boys than she would, I still love to get outside and play as well. We both want what's best for our boys! And, of course, you and your spouse want what's best for each other, for your kids, and for your family.

Andy Stanley says it well in his brilliant DVD series *Staying in Love*. In the *Staying in Love* discussion guide he writes, "We all face 'gaps' in our relationships where the other person doesn't fully meet our expectations. . . . We face the choice repeatedly in our marriages: Believe the best about our spouses (and see our love deepen); or assume the worst (and watch our love wither)."[1]

Those gaps are going to be there. They are part of life. They are certainly a part of married life—your marriage, my marriage, every marriage. When we face those gaps, we should practice the all-important command to submit to one another out of reverence for Christ—and to forget the scoreboard. It's not easy to do, but it's absolutely essential. When we choose to believe the best, when we truly forget the scoreboard, we live out the most important command for a covenant marriage. In fact, we exemplify to each other, to our kids, and to a watching world what Christian marriage is all about.

This is why (as I said in the introduction) we all need a Marriage Ref. And who is qualified to referee your marriage and mine? You have to go to the One who designed the game and wrote the rulebook. You have to go to the One who has told us how to have a healthy, functional marriage. Turn the page with me, and let's meet the Marriage Ref.

QUESTIONS FOR STUDY OR GROUP DISCUSSION

1 | Forget The Scoreboard

1. Has anyone ever given you a bad nickname or a bad reputation to live down like Touchdown Tony? How did that make you feel?

2. The biblical concept of mutual submission is based on humility—our deliberate choice to consider the needs and interests of others ahead of our own. Is submission easy or difficult for you? Explain your answer.

3. First Corinthians 13 describes Christlike covenant love as patient, kind, not envious, not boastful, not proud, not dishonoring toward others, unselfish, not easily angered, not grudge-bearing, not delighting in evil, rejoicing with the truth, protective, trusting, hopeful, persevering, and unfailing.

    - Which of these qualities best describes the way you love your spouse?

    - Which of these qualities least describes the way you love your spouse?

    - What specific action steps can you take, beginning this week, to become more complete in your covenant love toward your spouse?

4. The author describes six ways we tend to keep score in marriage: tallies, tone, tit-for-tat, facial ticks, taunting, and telling others. Which of these behaviors is your most serious problem area?

    - What specific action steps can you take this week to forget the scoreboard in your marriage?

5. Describe a time when you misjudged your spouse and later learned that you mistakenly believed the worst about your spouse. What did you learn from that experience?

    - What specific action steps can you take next time to be quick to forgive, quick to listen, quick to believe the best, and slow to judge your spouse?

2
THE MARRIAGE REF

I am NOT the Marriage Ref. And neither are you.

Don't get me wrong, I've tried to play the role of the Marriage Ref on many occasions. I even own a striped referee's jersey! I've tried to effectively play the Marriage Ref as a husband in my ten years of marriage to my beautiful wife Bridget, as a pastor at Neighborhood Church, and while offering wise counsel to friends who want advice, or couples in crisis. I can even offer sound, biblical advice amidst some dicey relational issues. Through the painful process of trial and error—and fifteen years of pastoral teaching and care—I have come to realize that, ultimately, the role of Marriage Ref is rightfully reserved for the One who created marriage.

I mentioned "trial and error." Here's an example. During the first year of marriage to Bridget, we were in a lively discussion about the manner in which her boss was mistreating her at the southern California chiropractic office they shared. For most of the conversation, we were on the same page— "fighting from the same corner," to use a boxing term. Yet, despite my positive intentions to protect my wife and provide encouraging counsel, at one point our conversation turned from teamwork to tussle. And I couldn't figure out what happened!

Upon further review, I realized the conversation turned south at precisely the moment I figuratively put on my Marriage Ref jersey, and got ready to blow the proverbial whistle. Bridget politely asked me to stop. She reminded me that she knew what needed to be done. She wanted to handle the situation in a manner she was comfortable with . . . and not exactly how I would choose to handle it. It wasn't a manner of right versus wrong, godly versus ungodly, or wise versus unwise. It was simply a matter of preference.

Here's the point: I tried to play Marriage Ref that time. And to be honest, that wasn't the only time I've figuratively put on that striped jersey. You (and your spouse) have probably have done the same thing at some point in your marriage. You may even own a ref's jersey! But whether you have a real jersey or not, you know what happens when you try to referee your own marriage.

So where can we go for guidance, direction, and fairness in the practical realm of the marriage relationship? Who can referee our disputes and enforce God's rules in a marriage? Because God loves us, He has laid out some simple guidelines for having a great marriage. Just like the rest of His loving guidelines, which function as gracious "guardrails" in our lives, His guidelines for marriage will bring blessing to your relationship.

Please don't miss what I'm saying about the timeless relevance of God's guidelines for your marriage: *If you follow His guidelines, you WILL be blessed!*

No more yellow cards

You may be a little disappointed to discover that *you* are not the Marriage Ref. There's something in all of us that wants to be the referee, the decider, the one in charge. There's something in all of us that envies the power of the referee.

In a basketball game, the referee blows his whistle and all action stops; everyone on both teams must do whatever the referee says. In a football game, the ref throws down a yellow flag, and the next words out of his mouth can send a team backward or forward five or ten yards or more. In a baseball game, the umpire and other officials determine whether a pitch is a ball or a strike, who is safe and who is out.

If you *really* want to see a ref who enjoys his work, watch an international soccer game. I love the way soccer referees deliver a yellow card. They seem to take sadistic pleasure in chastising players who commit a foul. When the ref spots an infraction, he pulls a yellow card from his pocket, turns to the crowd, and parades that card around for all to see. His body language says,

"Everybody look! He's getting a yellow card! He blew it! And I am calling him on it!"

And while the ref is parading that card around, the player runs up to the ref and argues his case. His body language says, "Are you kidding me? You can't be serious! I didn't do anything wrong!"

But the ref pointedly ignores the player's protests. He parades that yellow card around, and the player follows him, waving his arms and protesting his innocence. Will he change the ref's mind? Not a chance! Rules are rules. A yellow card is what it is—and if you collect enough yellows, the next one is red and you're out of the game.

There's a similar dynamic in marriage. As husbands, as wives, we don't like having our mistakes and faults pointed out, do we? When the Marriage Ref points out our fault, we're like that soccer player. We protest. We plead our case. We say, "I'm innocent!"

But the Marriage Ref wrote the rulebook. He knows if you're guilty or innocent—and the rules of marriage don't bend. You can't talk your way out of a yellow card. And if you collect enough yellows, the next one is red, and you just might find yourself ejected from the game of marriage. Tragically, it happens all the time.

It's a good thing God is the Marriage Ref, not us. Most of us, if we got a chance to referee our own marriages, would be very quick to pull that yellow card. We'd hold up that card and say, "Everybody look! My spouse is getting a yellow card! My partner blew it! Foul! Foul!"

In fact, many of us *do* set ourselves up as the Marriage Ref. We act as if we have the right to pull that yellow card—and we keep it hair-triggered, don't we? No more yellow cards. No more red cards. No more acting like the referee of your own marriage. It's time to listen to the One who truly has the right to be called the Marriage Ref.

Guard your heart

This book isn't really designed to be read. It's an interactive book. I invite you to live in these pages, wrestle with the questions at the end of each chapter, write down your own honest answers, and discuss your answers with your spouse or a discussion group. As you read, feel free to underline, highlight, and write notes in the margins. Avoid the temptation to answer questions on behalf of your spouse. The only person you can fix is you.

As you and your spouse go through this book together, you'll come across some point, some principle, some example, and you'll really hope that your spouse *gets* it. You'll be tempted to underscore that point for the benefit of your marriage partner: "Hmmm, look at *this* paragraph! Boy, it really rings true, doesn't it? I wonder if *you* can relate to what he's saying here . . ." Or, if you think you're being *really* clever and subtle, you might try to get your point across with a raised eyebrow, a little sigh, or even a nudge of the elbow in your spouse's ribs.

Please don't. You know where that temptation comes from, don't you? It comes from that sneaky part of you that wants to be the Marriage Ref. We need to rely on the Holy Spirit to make His truth known where it is needed. Our job is to focus on what the Marriage Ref is saying to us, not to anyone else.

In John 21:18-22, there's a scene in which the apostle Peter is walking with the risen Lord, and Jesus tells Peter that he will one day die a martyr's death. Then Peter turns and sees John following them a few paces behind. "Lord," Peter says, "what about him?" And Jesus tells Peter, in essence, "Don't worry about God's will for John. Just stay focused on God's will for *your* life. God's will for John is between God and John. You must follow me."

And our Lord has the same counsel for you and me. It's not my job to make sure that my wife Bridget is listening to God and doing His will. I have a fulltime job just making sure that *I'm* listening to God and doing His will for *my* life. God's will for Bridget is between God and Bridget. I must follow Jesus, and let God deal with Bridget.

As you read through this book, trust the Holy Spirit to speak to your mate. Ask God to speak to you about your own faults and flaws. Ask Him to remove the blinders from your own eyes. As you begin this study, go to God in prayer, acknowledge Him as the Marriage Ref in your life. Ask Him to show you your yellow card. Ask Him to reveal to you His rulebook for a strong and healthy marriage.

If you focus on the condition of your own heart, I believe you'll see growth and improvement in your relationship that will astound you. But if you yield to the temptation to become the Marriage Ref in your own marriage, then you'll probably just bring harm to your relationship.

Proverbs 4:23 tells us, "Above all else, guard your heart, for everything you do flows from it." Some translations use the word "keep" or "watch" instead of "guard." This verse is not telling us to guard our hearts in a protective sense. It's not telling us that we should build a wall around our hearts. Rather, it means that we are to carefully watch what comes in and what goes out of our hearts. It means that we are to monitor the thoughts and behavior of our innermost being. Guard your heart because it is the wellspring of your life—and your marriage relationship.

The key word for applying this passage is "your." You are to guard *your* heart, not someone else's, not the heart of your marriage partner. That doesn't come naturally to us, does it? We'd much rather pull a yellow card on someone else than accept a yellow card on ourselves. And I include myself in that indictment.

I'm rarely aware of the fouls I've committed in my own marriage unless someone else catches me and points them out to me. I'm often oblivious to the wrongs I commit unless Bridget says, "Honey, that was hurtful," or until a friend in my accountability group takes me aside and says, "Tyler, did you stop and consider how Bridget would feel when you said that?"

Just as you can't see the spinach in your teeth without a mirror, you often can't see the harm you're doing in your marriage until someone reflects your actions back to you. So drop your defenses. Invite your spouse and your most trusted friends to tell you when your words and behavior are hurtful and inappropriate.

Take a look in the mirror. Reflect on yourself, your behavior, your relationships, and the way you interact with your marriage partner.

If you are not married

I have not written this book only for married couples. In fact, I hope many unmarried people read it, especially those who are thinking of marriage and planning for marriage. When I first gave this series of talks on marriage, I asked for a show of hands, and I found that about two-thirds of my audience was married, and about one-third unmarried. Statistically, more than nine out of ten people will get married at some point in their lives.

If you are not yet married, wouldn't you like to know the guidelines for a happy and healthy marriage relationship from the start? Wouldn't you rather go into marriage knowing God's plan for marriage instead of finding out too late that you *missed* His plan?

You might say, "That's well and good. But I'm not really interested in knowing more about marriage relationships right now. Marriage isn't on my radar right now. I'm still enjoying my singleness. I'm going to put this book aside and check out of this conversation."

Not so fast. You're assuming that God's teaching about marriage in the Bible is all about you and your needs. It's not. The Bible doesn't merely teach these principles so that you can be happy in your marriage—although the Bible does contain the principles for a happy marriage. God has a deeper reason for teaching us His design and plan for marriage.

The marriage relationship between a man and a woman is the highest, deepest, most intimate human relationship on earth. No other human relationship remotely compares to the depth of intimacy between a husband and wife in a marriage. And there's a good reason for that.

The marriage relationship is the *one* relationship above all others that depicts God's relationship with us. Again and again in the Bible, God likens

His relationship with us to the relationship between a husband and wife. As Paul writes to the Ephesians:

> Husbands, love your wives, just as Christ loved the church and gave himself up for her to make her holy, cleansing her by the washing with water through the word, and to present her to himself as a radiant church, without stain or wrinkle or any other blemish, but holy and blameless. . . . "For this reason a man will leave his father and mother and be united to his wife, and the two will become one flesh." This is a profound mystery—but I am talking about Christ and the church (Ephesians 5:25-27, 31-32).

The marriage relationship, writes Paul, is a picture of the relationship between Christ and the church. Whether you are married, going to be married, or never to be married, it's important to understand God's truth for His church, as revealed through the biblical model of marriage. God's principles for a healthy marriage are not intended merely as a guide to a happier marriage, but as the key to understanding our faith and our relationship with God.

I recently officiated at the wedding of some friends who are not yet followers of Christ. Generally, I meet with a couple several times to provide pastoral counseling, to help them prepare for marriage, and to go over all the details for their Big Day. One of my favorite parts of the premarital counseling process is the night I walk the couple through this amazing passage of Scripture on marriage, Ephesians 5:21-33. In the course of that conversation, I explain the cultural context into which Paul was writing, the simple principles of love and respect, and how the sacrificing, pursuing, nourishing, cherishing love of a husband is a beautiful picture of the love Jesus Christ has for us—His Bride.

As I went through the discussion with this couple, I experienced one of those precious "God moments." I saw a light bulb go on in the minds and hearts of this couple. No, they didn't suddenly fall to their knees and receive Jesus as the Lord of their lives. But their hearts definitely softened to the Gospel that day. They thought deeply about the relentless tenderness of Jesus' love for them. They listened. And their eyes glistened at the idea of *their* marriage serving as an image before other people, depicting the reality of God's covenant love.

For them, seeing that picture and understanding the power of God's design for marriage was the first step toward enjoying their *own* relationship with God—and a happier, healthier marriage.

My prayer is that you and your marriage partner will have this same experience in your own marriage.

QUESTIONS FOR STUDY OR GROUP DISCUSSION

2 | The Marriage Ref

1. Have you ever thought about why you decided to get married?

    - What purpose do you think God has for your marriage?

2. Have you ever tried to be the "marriage ref" in your own marriage?

    - How did that turn out?

    - What could (or should) you have done differently?

3. The author writes: "*Just as you can't see the spinach in your teeth without a mirror, you can't see the harm you're doing in your marriage until someone reflects your actions back to you. So drop your defenses. Invite your spouse and your most trusted friends to tell you when your words and behavior are hurtful and inappropriate.*"

    - Do you have friends in your life who will hold you accountable for your words and behavior toward your spouse?

- If not, why not? Is there anything that prevents you from asking a few trusted friends to hold you accountable?

4. The Bible likens the marriage relationship to the relationship between Christ and the church. What does your marriage say to you about the relationship between Christ and His people?

- How would your marriage need to change in order to be a better example of the relationship between Christ and the church?

3
THE MARRIAGE COVENANT

The traditional marriage vows focus on a promise to love, honor, and cherish each other "as long as we both shall live." In some non-traditional wedding ceremonies today, however, that phrase has been replaced by a promise that reflects the commitment-phobic age in which we live—a promise to love, honor, and cherish "as long as we both shall *love*."

What was once a solemn vow to love until death has become a mutual agreement to love until the love dies. In other words, "I promise to love you as long as I *feel* like loving you." That's not much of a promise, is it?

In our culture today, it's easier to walk away from a marriage contract than it is to cancel the contract with your fitness gym. In fact, marriage is sometimes called "the least binding of all contracts." What a sad commentary on the state of marriage today!

Many people refer to marriage as "a piece of paper." They say, "All that matters is that we love each other. We don't need a piece of paper to prove our love." This statement misses the point of marriage. A marriage covenant doesn't take place when two people sign their names to a piece of paper. A covenant is not the same thing as a contract. Two people may not need a piece of paper to prove their love, but they do need a covenant to ensure that their love will last for life.

Just as every building needs a strong foundation to ensure its structural integrity, every marriage needs a strong foundation. That foundation is the marriage covenant. Without the foundation of a covenant, a marriage is unlikely to stand the test of time, the test of adversity, and the ups and downs of human emotion.

A contract says, "This relationship is fifty-fifty." A covenant says, "I commit myself to you one-hundred percent." A contract says, "We have a deal." A covenant says, "We have a relationship." Whether you see your marriage as a contract or a covenant makes all the difference in how you relate to your marriage partner—and how hard you will work to make your marriage last. Covenant marriage is the only kind of marriage that truly honors God and exemplifies His relationship with humanity.

What is a covenant relationship?

How does a covenant relationship differ from all other relationships? Let's explore the covenant love of Jesus and apply His covenant love to the marriage relationship. Jesus referred to the "new covenant" in Luke 22:20, during the Last Supper with His disciples, when He told them, "This cup is the new covenant in my blood, which is poured out for you." Note that phrase: *the new covenant of my blood.*

The same night He spoke those words, Jesus was betrayed and went to the cross. Through His death on the cross, He ushered in the era of the new covenant. The book of Hebrews tells us that "Christ is the mediator of a new covenant, that those who are called may receive the promised eternal inheritance" (Hebrews 9:15). And the apostle Paul tells us that God has "made us competent as ministers of a new covenant" (2 Corinthians 3:6).

In order to fully appreciate the meaning of this new covenant, we need to understand what the old covenant meant. The old covenant first began to take shape in Genesis 2. There, God makes a covenant with Adam in language that is strong, clear, and definitive:

> The LORD God took the man and put him in the Garden of Eden to work it and take care of it. And the LORD God commanded the man, "You are free to eat from any tree in the garden; but you must not eat from the tree of the knowledge of good and evil, for when you eat from it you will certainly die" (Genesis 2:15-17).

This is covenant language. God says, in effect, "I will give you this, and if you keep the conditions of this covenant, I will do these things for you—but if you violate the conditions of this covenant, you will suffer certain consequences." That's God's covenant with Adam in Genesis 2. In Genesis 3, we see that the covenant involves Eve as well:

> The woman said to the serpent, "We may eat fruit from the trees in the garden, but God did say, 'You must not eat fruit from the tree that is in the middle of the garden, and you must not touch it, or you will die'" (Genesis 3:2-3).

From the covenant with Adam and Eve, we move through the Old Testament and we see God making different types of covenants. He makes a covenant with Noah, with Abraham, with Moses, with David—and each of these Old Testament covenants anticipates the *ultimate* covenant, the *new* covenant, as it would be established and secured through the blood of Jesus Christ.

What is a covenant? To define it simply, *a covenant is a binding relationship based on a promise.* The Old Testament covenants were more than mere contracts. They were *relationships* founded on God's promises. Even the Old Testament speaks of the new covenant of the blood of Jesus Christ. In Jeremiah 31, God says, in effect, "Yes, we have all of these old covenants of the Old Testament, but there is a new covenant coming. There is a new binding relationship coming, and it will be based on a new promise." The prophet Jeremiah writes:

> "The days are coming," declares the LORD,
>   "when I will make a new covenant
> with the people of Israel
>   and with the people of Judah.
> It will not be like the covenant

> I made with their ancestors
> when I took them by the hand
> to lead them out of Egypt,
> because they broke my covenant,
> though I was a husband to them,"
> declares the LORD.
> "This is the covenant I will make with the people of Israel
> after that time," declares the LORD.
> "I will put my law in their minds
> and write it on their hearts.
> I will be their God,
> and they will be my people.
> No longer will they teach their neighbor,
> or say to one another, 'Know the LORD,'
> because they will all know me,
> from the least of them to the greatest,"
> declares the LORD.
> "For I will forgive their wickedness
> and will remember their sins no more" (Jeremiah 31:31-34).

Now, this is a fascinating passage—and at this point, you may be getting a hint of why, in this book about marriage relationships, we're taking the time to look at the old covenant and new covenant relationships in the Bible. Notice that God said to the people of Israel, "I was a husband to them." God pictures His relationship to His people as being like a marriage relationship.

This wife, the nation of Israel, has been unfaithful to her husband, the Lord God. So God now says to his unfaithful wife, "This is the covenant I will make with the people of Israel.... I will put my law in their minds and write it on their hearts. I will be their God, and they will be my people.... For I will forgive their wickedness and will remember their sins no more."

Through this new covenant, God promises to forgive and restore His unfaithful wife. There are two ways to read this passage in Jeremiah. Either you will read it with the mindset of a lawyer, noticing the legal clauses, the references to covenants and laws—or you read it with the mindset of a lover, noticing the tender references to an intimate relationship, and to the promise of forgiveness and reconciliation. This passage contains both lawyerly language and love language.

I have found that most people tend to approach relationship problems in one of two ways: in a lawyerly way or a loving way. I have read this passage to an audience and have asked for a show of hands: "How many of you see this as a lawyerly passage of Scripture? And how many of you see this as a love passage of Scripture?" It probably wouldn't surprise you that most of the men in the audience tended to fall into the "lawyer" category, while most of the women tended to fall into the "lover" category.

There are certainly exceptions to every generalization, but I find that, on the whole, men tend to think like lawyers and women tend to think like lovers. Men tend to focus on requirements and rules and consequences. Women tend to focus on relationships and feelings and connection.

So this would be a good time to ask yourself: Do I approach life as more of a lawyer—or as more of a lover?

The perfect blending of law and love

A legal contract is an agreement between two or more parties that is enforceable by law. A covenant is much more than a contract. A covenant is a relationship—a binding relationship based on a promise. It is the *relationship* that distinguishes a covenant from a contract.

My friend Kevin is a real estate attorney. I once asked him, "Kevin, what do you think of when I say the word 'covenant'?"

He said, "I immediately think of 'CC&Rs,' which means covenants, conditions, and restrictions. It's a legal term."

It's true. In a strictly legal sense, a covenant refers to terms and conditions that must be met or else a law penalty must be paid. There are rewards and benefits for obeying covenants, conditions, and restrictions, and there are penalties—you might even call them "curses"—for disobeying. These legal rewards and legal penalties are what make a covenant meaningful. They hold both parties accountable for abiding by the terms of the covenant.

All contracts have a lawyerly dimension. But when we see the word "covenant" in the Bible, there is an added dimension of relationship, of love, of intimacy and feelings and connection. A biblical covenant is both law and love. A covenant has the force of law, but it also has the power of love. A covenant is more intimate and loving than a mere legal agreement, and it is more binding and abiding then a relationship based only on affection.

What happens if you remove the legal dimension of the covenant, and leave only the love? Many people do that today. These are the couples who say, "We don't need a piece of paper to prove we love each other." So they decide to live together, relying on love alone to keep them together. And they generally define "love" as a passionate and tender emotion they feel for each other.

But a marriage covenant has a dimension that loving emotions don't provide—a dimension of *accountability*. Emotions rise and fall, but a marriage covenant is based on a promise, on marriage vows. Two people in a marriage covenant are accountable to keep those vows *regardless of their emotions in any particular moment*. So when emotions alone aren't enough to hold a marriage together, the marriage vows hold both partners accountable. The covenant binds them together until the emotions of love are restored.

A covenant relationship is stronger than law alone—and it is stronger than love alone. That's because a covenant is *both* law and love. According to God's Word, a covenant is the highest and finest type of relationship we could possibly experience. That's why God initiates covenant relationships with us in both the Old and New Testaments.

This is also why, throughout the Bible, God likens His relationship with us to a marriage relationship between a man and a woman. His relationship with us is the perfect blending of both law and love.

When you look at the covenants God initiates between Himself and His people in the Old Testament, the first language we hear is the language of love. It's the language of intimacy. We hear it in God's use of personal possessive pronouns in describing His relationship with His people. He says, "I will be your God and you will be my people."

I perform a lot of weddings, and my favorite part of the wedding ceremony is where the bride and groom exchange marriage vows. The first line of each vow is deeply personal and deeply possessive. The groom looks into the eyes of his bride and says (as I once said to my bride), "I, Tyler, take you, Bridget, to be my wife." And the groom makes a series of promises that form the foundation of his relationship to her.

Then, the bride looks into the eyes of her husband, and she says (as Bridget once said to me), "I, Bridget, take you, Tyler, to be my husband." Once again, her words are deeply personal and deeply possessive—and then she makes promises to him.

In this exchange of vows, the bride and groom speak to each other in the intimate language of love. Then they make promises to each other—they make a covenant with each other in the sight of many witnesses. This covenant becomes the protective enclosure that will enable them to maintain their relationship safely and securely for as long as they both shall live.

God's perplexing instructions

The key to appreciating the new covenant love of God is an understanding of how Jesus Christ fulfills the old covenant conditions set forth in the Old Testament. We find those old covenant conditions in Deuteronomy 28, where God says to Israel:

> If you fully obey the LORD your God and carefully follow all his commands I give you today, the LORD your God will set you high above all the nations on earth. All these blessings will come

on you and accompany you if you obey the LORD your God (Deuteronomy 28:1-2).

Then God sets forth a series of blessings that will follow in exchange for Israel's obedience. In addition to the blessings for obedience, God also spells out consequences (or "curses") for disobedience:

However, if you do not obey the LORD your God and do not carefully follow all his commands and decrees I am giving you today, all these curses will come on you and overtake you (Deuteronomy 28:15).

And God goes on to list those consequences or "curses." And here many people have a problem with believing God and understanding the old covenant. First, in verses 1-14, God lists the blessings, which include prosperity, bountiful rains and rich harvests, honor and respect among nations, victory over enemies, and more. Here, God is love.

But in verses 15-68, God pronounces a series of curses that will fall on Israel if the people disobey and break the covenant. Here, God is law. So we read this passage and we are confused. We ask, "Is God law—or is He love? Are His blessings conditional or unconditional?"

It's as if there are two opposite ways of looking at God. I have to confess that there are times in my life when I find myself in one camp or the other. I find the blessings to be more conditional, more a matter of law, on some days, and more unconditional, more a matter of love, on others. How do we resolve this seeming contradiction between a God of love and a God of law?

That's one of the most fundamental questions of the Bible. All through Scripture, you find God saying, "I will bless you, I will love you, I will pursue you, I have great plans for you"—and right there on the very same page you also find, "But listen to me, obey me, I am a just God, I cannot bless a disobedient people." Is this a contradiction?

In Genesis 15, the Lord made His covenant with Abraham. This scene enables us to see whether God is law or love, justice or mercy. In that passage, God comes to Abraham (or Abram, as his name was at that time) in a vision. God tells him, in effect, "I will bless you, I will give you a son, and I will bless all the nations through that son. Wait for me."

Now, Abraham was already far along in age, probably 99 years old. And this old man asks God a question I think we've all asked at one point or another in our lives: "How can I know?" Like Abraham, we've all wondered; "How can I know that God exists? How can I know He cares about me? How can I know that His promises are trustworthy?"

And God's answer to Abraham was essentially this: "There's a lot you can't know—but let me tell you something you *can* know. Abraham, come out of your tent. Look up at the sky and count the stars. So shall your offspring be." And the Scriptures tell us that Abraham believed God, and God counted Abraham's faith as if it were righteousness.

Then God gave Abraham a set of perplexing instructions. He told Abraham to kill a number of animals, cut the carcasses in half, and arrange the two halves opposite each other with room to walk in between. These instructions seem gruesome to us today. But the people of Abraham's day were familiar with this ritual. God was preparing to establish a covenant with Abraham according to the customs of Abraham's culture.

The parties to the covenant would sacrifice the animals and lay one half here and the other half there. The person who dictated terms of the covenant was the "head" of the covenant—and in this case, the head of the covenant is God. Traditionally, the two parties to the covenant—in this case, God and Abraham—would then walk between the divided carcasses. This symbolized the act of stepping into the covenant relationship with each other.

By walking between the pieces of the slain animals, the parties to the covenant were walking between the blood. In an ancient culture, that is how you form the covenant. You literally "cut" a covenant. That's where we get the phrase "let's cut a deal." In ancient times, you couldn't just shake on it. You had to cut a covenant, because there had to be blood to seal the covenant. A blood "curse" signified the consequences of breaking the covenant.

When the parties to the covenant walked between the pieces of bloodied animal flesh, they were saying, in effect, "I will fulfill this covenant—and if I break it, may I be cut into bloody pieces like these dismembered animals."

When God commanded Abraham to cut up the animals, Abraham understood the symbolism. He believed that both he and God would walk between the carcasses, and this ceremony would establish the covenant between them. Abraham expected that God would say, "Hold up your end of the covenant, Abraham, and I'll hold up mine." But that's not what happened.

Abraham waited for God. And he waited and he waited. He had to chase off birds of prey that came to feed on the carcasses. Finally, Abraham fell asleep—and a great darkness came over him. And God spoke to Abraham and made promises to him. A blazing torch appeared out of the darkness and passed between the animal pieces.

But Abraham himself did not walk between the pieces of animal flesh—only the torch of God Himself. Why didn't Abraham have to walk between the animal pieces?

Torn to pieces

Every detail of this story is significant. God caused Abraham to fall asleep, and God didn't let Abraham walk between the pieces. When God passed between the pieces in the form of a fiery torch, he was saying, in effect, "*I alone* will fulfill the terms of this covenant—and if the terms of this covenant are broken, *may this happen to Me*. I will be cut to pieces if I don't fulfill the promises of this covenant—and I will be cut to pieces if *you* don't fulfill the promises of this covenant."

God alone makes this vow. He alone sets the conditions of the covenant—and he alone takes the curse of breaking the covenant. His message to

Abraham—and to you and to me—is, "I will bless you. I will pursue you. I will forgive you. I will always be here for you even if it means that I, the Lord Almighty, have to clothe my immortality with mortality. I will keep my covenant with you *even if I have to literally be torn to pieces*—because you don't know how to fulfill your end of the covenant."

And here is the amazing news: He *was* torn to pieces!

Centuries after God made that covenant with Abraham, darkness covered a hill called Calvary, and God the Father looked down on God the Son, and the Father watched His only Son being torn to bloody pieces by a Roman scourge and a crown of thorns, by nails in His hands and feet, by a spear in his side. Jesus took the covenant curse.

God kept His covenant with Abraham, knowing full well that Abraham and all human beings were incapable of keeping the covenant. God, through His Son, allowed himself to be torn to pieces—not because *He* broke the covenant, but because *we* did. He knew we couldn't keep our end of the bargain, so he said, "I'll do it for you. I'll pay the debt you can never repay." God fulfilled both the old covenant and the new covenant.

So is God's love conditional—or is it unconditional? Is God law or is God love?

The answer is, "Yes!"

Yes, His love is conditional. And yes, His love is unconditional. We could not meet His conditions, so in His unconditional love, He met the conditions for us. We could not live up to God's law, so in His love, He paid the legal penalty for us.

Jesus Christ, through His perfect life and sinless obedience, fulfilled the conditions of the covenant. His sacrificial death fulfilled the demands of the curse that were laid upon us when we broke the covenant.

The covenant contains conditions, blessings, and curses. We failed to meet the conditions, so Jesus took our curse upon Himself. But who gets the blessing? Answer: We do!

Jesus lived a perfect life. He died a painful death. He went to the cross and paid for our sin. He took our curse upon Himself. Now, you and I can have the blessing. We can have a relationship with God through the new covenant love of Jesus.[1]

The husband and the adulterous wife

That is the heart of the Gospel. That is the covenant love of God, as He expressed it to us in the old covenant with Abraham and in the new covenant through Jesus Christ. You may think, "Okay, thanks for the theology lesson, Tyler. But I thought this was a book about marriage. What does all this have to do with my marriage?"

Actually, it has everything to do with marriage. God pictures his relationship to us through the symbols of covenant marriage. Jesus says to us, "I am the bridegroom and you are my bride. I am standing here at the altar, ready to place the ring upon your finger and possess you forever as my bride. I know that you have betrayed me in the past. I know you will cheat on me in the future. But I love you so much that I will marry you anyway."

Jesus, the bridegroom, pursues us even while we reject Him. He has pursued us all the way to the cross. He forgives us even while we are sinning against Him. He says to us, "I love you. Nothing you do can change that. No matter how you have hurt me and rejected me and trampled on my love for you, I will marry you anyway."

And once you begin to appreciate all that Jesus has suffered and forgiven in order to win you as His bride, you begin to understand how to live out covenant love and covenant forgiveness in your own marriage. You learn to apply Christlike covenant love to every situation in your life. And that is how you build a marriage that lasts a lifetime—and a marriage that reflects the covenant love of Jesus Christ.

The Old Testament book of Hosea tells the story of the prophet Hosea, who lived during the time when Israel had horribly betrayed God and His covenant. The people of Israel had turned away from God to serve Baal, the false god of the Canaanites. Sins of murder, perjury, theft, and sexual debauchery were rampant throughout Israel. So God instructed Hosea to show the people of Israel what His love for them was truly like.

God told Hosea, "Go, marry a promiscuous woman and have children with her, for like an adulterous wife this land is guilty of unfaithfulness to the LORD" (Hosea 1:2). So Hosea married a prostitute named Gomer and she had children with him. Eventually, Gomer became restless and unhappy in her role as the prophet's wife. She left Hosea and went back to her life of prostitution and adultery.

So God spoke to Hosea again and said, "Go, show your love to your wife again, though she is loved by another man and is an adulteress. Love her as the LORD loves the Israelites, though they turn to other gods . . ." (Hosea 3:1). So Hosea went out and found his wife in the arms of another man, and he bought her for fifteen pieces of silver. Then he took her home, forgave her, and renewed his wedding vows with her.

God uses marriage to picture his relationship with the human race. Even though we have turned away from God and cheated on Him, He loves us, He pursues us, and He purchases us with a great price. Through His covenant love for us, God shows us what our covenant marriage relationship should look like. And through our covenant marriage, we demonstrate to the world the power of His covenant love.

QUESTIONS FOR STUDY OR GROUP DISCUSSION

3 | The Marriage Covenant

1. Do you see your marriage as a contractual agreement or as a covenant? Explain your answer.

2. What do you see as the foundation of your marriage? In other words, what is the "glue" that holds your marriage relationship together? Try to state the honest answer, as you truly see it—not necessarily the answer the author suggests. If you believe your marriage relationship is founded on something other than a covenant, what would that foundation be?

   - Do you see the foundation of your marriage as essentially firm, secure, and healthy? Explain your answer.

   - What steps (if any) would you and your marriage partner need to take to make your marriage what you truly want it to be?

3. When you read the verses from Jeremiah 31, did you read them with the mindset of a lawyer—or a lover? Explain your answer.

4. Do you approach most problems and situations in your marriage with the mindset of a lawyer—or a lover? Explain your answer.

5. The author says that God's love is both conditional and unconditional, both law and love. Do you agree or disagree? Explain your answer.

- Does this discussion of God's law and God's love change your view of God? In what way?

4
COVENANT RELATIONSHIP— OR CONSUMER RELATIONSHIP?

I'm in a relationship with my fitness gym.

My health is important to me and I like to work out. So I have a membership with Bally Total Fitness. There is only one reason I chose Bally Total Fitness over all the gyms in my local area: Convenience. It's closer to my house than any other gym.

Do I have relationships with the *people* at Bally Total Fitness? You bet I do. I know all the people at the front desk. I know the people who work in the child care center. And I know most of the clients of the gym, the people I regularly work out with, by name.

But I confess that if there were a Bally Total Fitness or a 24-Hour Fitness or a Club Sport—you name it—that was closer to my house, I would leave my current gym in a heartbeat and join the gym that was closer to my house. I have a relationship with my fitness gym—but it's not a covenant relationship. It's a *consumer* relationship.

I have no covenant with those people. My gym membership is purely a business arrangement. I pay the gym a certain amount of money, and in exchange for that money the gym lets me use its facilities and equipment. I go there to work out and sweat and burn calories, and I want the whole arrangement to be as convenient as possible.

I have a similar relationship with my coffee shop. A lot of people like Starbucks. Many other people prefer the little independent mom-and-pop coffee shops. But I happen to love Peet's Coffee. I love the wonderful people who work there. They brew up the coffee that awakens my brain and caffeinates my day. But I'm not in a covenant relationship with the baristas at Peet's.

There are several Peet's Coffee locations near me. There's one near the church where at work. There's another one right around the corner from my house. When I want coffee, I go to whichever Peet's location is closest. I have no particular loyalty to one Peet's shop versus another. Why? Because I don't have a covenant relationship with Peet's Coffee. As much as I love that wonderful brew, my relationship with Peet's is purely a consumer relationship.

Not all of our relationships are covenant relationships. Many are consumer relationships—and that's okay. Healthy consumer relationships make for a vibrant economy and a prosperous society. Consumer relationships are a good thing.

Where we run into trouble is when we bring consumer attitudes into covenant relationships. You might think that's a ridiculous notion. No one would ever treat a marriage partner as you would treat your fitness gym or your coffee shop! But you'd be surprised at how many married people take consumer tendencies into covenant territory with disastrous results. In fact, you might be having a consumer relationship with your own marriage partner right now and not even realize it.

What are consumer attitudes?

There is no deeper, more satisfying relationship in all of human experience than a covenant relationship—a binding relationship based on a promise, a relationship bound by both law and love. So when we begin bringing consumer attitudes into a covenant relationship, an alarm should sound! Consumer tendencies are deadly to covenant relationships.

What are consumer attitudes? They are attitudes that focus more on what I *get from* a relationship than what I can *give to* it. They are attitudes that focus on *my* wants, *my* needs, *my* convenience, *my* advantage.

Consumers don't think about what's best for Wal-Mart or Starbucks or General Motors. If the items I want are cheaper, the store closer, and the checkout lines shorter at Target, I don't owe any allegiance to Wal-Mart. If I prefer Peet's over Starbucks—if I think it's kind of dumb that "tall" means small and "grande" means medium and "venti" means huge—then I'm sticking with Peet's. If I know that General Motors is struggling financially, I don't feel a covenant obligation to buy my next car from GM in order to help out the company. As a smart consumer, I'm going to buy the car that offers the best style, price, fuel economy, safety, and quality I can find.

A consumer attitude always asks, "What will make me happy?" If I get high value at a low price, I'm happy. If the consumer transaction is quick and convenient, I'm even happier. If I can't get the value, price, and convenience that makes me happy at Store X, then my consumer relationship with that store is over, and I'm going across the street to Store Y.

Now, what happens when we take this attitude into our covenant relationships? We stop asking our marriage partner, "How can I make *you* happy?" We start focusing on, "Why don't you make *me* happy?" Instead of looking for all of our marriage partner's endearing and pleasing traits, we start noticing faults and flaws. Our consumer mentality tells us that this "product" we married may not be as good as we once thought, and we may even start "comparison shopping" as we did before we got married. We look around at the office, or down the street, or even at church, and think, "What if I had married him instead?" or "I wonder how life would be with her instead?"

That is consumer thinking. And consumer attitudes are deadly to a covenant marriage.

Our family, our failures and our future

How do we apply these principles in our everyday lives? How can we learn to shed our consumer thinking when it comes to marriage and family? How do we learn to start thinking about our relationships in a covenantal way? Let me suggest four ways that we can apply covenant love and make covenant relationships a reality in our lives. We can apply covenant love in these four arenas of life: our *families*, our *future*, our *failures*, and our *faithfulness*.

To begin, let's apply the principles of covenant love to our *families*.

I'm in a covenant marriage with my wife Bridget. This means I turn consumer thinking completely around. Consumer thinking is focused on pleasing myself. Covenant thinking is focused on pleasing Bridget. Once I begin training myself, reminding myself, and motivating myself to think about ways to make Bridget happy, I find myself thinking less and less about what makes Tyler happy. I find myself feeling convicted when I fail her, when I sin against her, when I behave selfishly toward her. That conviction comes from an awareness that selflessness is the key to a covenant relationship—and selfishness is a poison that kills covenant relationships.

Because our marriage is a covenant relationship, Bridget and I are committed to remaining together and serving each other throughout our lives. She will never leave me and I will never leave her—ever! Why? Because God has shown us what covenant relationships are all about. My Lord has promised never to leave me, so I will never leave Bridget.

We are also in covenant relationships as parents. Our three boys, Trevor, Owen, and Cole, know they can trust the love that Mom and Dad have for them, because it is covenant love. They hear this message from us again and again: "We love you, we will always love you, and there is nothing you could ever do that would make us stop loving you. We are locked in a covenant-love-tight relationship."

When I practice covenant love in my family, when I truly love Bridget and my three boys, when I pursue them and give myself to them unselfishly, when I am always there for them and never forsake them, then my love for them reflects the covenant love God has for me. My highest hope for my three boys is not that they would get straight A's (though I hope they will always achieve their God-given potential), and not that they play professional sports (though I would certainly be their biggest fan). My highest hope for them is that they would anchor their souls in the one thing that is firm and secure and eternal: A covenant love relationship with the Lord Jesus Christ.

One way I can influence my boys to place their trust in Jesus is by modeling Christlike covenant love toward them on a consistent basis. And I also know that if I violate that trust, if I damage their ability to trust, I place a huge roadblock in their path, making it harder for them to place their faith and trust in Jesus.

That is how we apply covenant love to our families. Now, let's apply the principles of covenant love to our *failures*.

One Sunday morning at 6 a.m., I went to Peet's for coffee and some quiet time to go over my notes for teaching later that day at church. I had a really good time of study, and I was all fired up. After finishing my coffee, I drove home to pick up Bridget and the boys to go to church. I strode into the house all full of pep and caffeine, and shouted, "Okay, let's go! Let's go!"

But the boys weren't ready, and I had to wait a few minutes. And as I waited, all of my pep and enthusiasm turned to impatience and frustration. "Let's go! Let's go!" I said—but now I was growling with annoyance. By the time we all piled into the car, I had totally lost my temper. I was yelling at my wife. I was yelling at my kids.

At a stoplight, I turned around and looked at all the faces in the car—and everybody had tears in their eyes! And it was all because of me!

I had sinned against my wife. I had sinned against my children. Instantly, I knew that I had violated my covenant love for my family. I had violated the example of a Christlike loving father. I knew what had to do—so I asked Bridget and my three boys to forgive me. And they did.

The greatest model of parent-child love is the covenant relationship God has with all of us as His children. Jesus described that relationship in his story of The Loving Father and the Prodigal Son (see Luke 15:11-32). The loving father in that story is the model of loving fatherhood that I measure myself against every day. When I fall short of that example, as I did that Sunday morning, I have to go to my family and say, "I failed. I blew it. I wasn't practicing covenant love just now. Please forgive me." And because of their covenant love for me, they do. They forgive me every time.

Covenant forgiveness is not "cheap grace." The love and forgiveness of Jesus Christ may be free to me, but it came at an infinite and ultimate cost to Jesus Himself. He had to give his life in order for my sins to be forgiven. On the cross, He became both my justice and my mercy.

We all need to look squarely at our failures. I need to look at mine. You need to look at yours. We all have them, and they are painful to admit. But the good news is that our sin has been paid for.

That's how we apply covenant love to our failures. Now let's apply the principles of covenant love to our *faithfulness*.

Once we understand covenant love, it totally transforms our motivation for obeying God, for remaining faithful and true to God throughout our lives. Many people are "religious" and try to live "good lives" in order to earn favor with God. But once we understand covenant love, we realize there's no way we can earn favor with God by our own works. Jesus Christ did all of the work, and all we can do is accept His perfect work upon the cross on our behalf.

If we accept His covenant love for us, expressed to us through the death and resurrection of Jesus Christ, we no longer try to earn God's favor. We have already received God's favor, His grace, and His love. Now, instead of obeying out of fear or the hope of reward, we obey out of thankfulness and gratitude. Our salvation is not based on our church attendance or how much money we gave. It's not based on whether we've remembered to cross every "t" and dot every "i." It's not based on our performance at all.

Instead, God says to us, "I accept you based on what *I* have done. I have inaugurated a new covenant with you. Don't obey in order to be accepted. You are already accepted, so obey. This is your loving and thankful response to me."

Outwardly, a person who is trying to earn acceptance from God by good works may not seem any different from the person who obeys God out of sheer gratitude and covenant love. But inwardly, the difference between these two people is like night and day. The person who tries to earn God's acceptance always wonders, "Have I done enough?" The person who obeys God out of gratitude prays, "Lord, I can never do enough to repay you, but I will spend the rest of my life serving you and obeying you out of gratitude for your amazing covenant love."

We've discussed applying God's covenant love to our families, and our failures. Now let's apply His covenant love to our *future*.

Our future is full of uncertainty. We face insecurities about our health, our careers, the global economy, and many other factors in our lives. Tragedy could crash into our lives at any moment without warning. Life is uncertain—and in the midst of the insecurity and instability of this life, only one thing is firm and secure: Our covenant relationship with God.

The Lord Jesus tells us that His unchanging love for us is our one and only anchor of security in a sea of uncertainty. He tells us, in effect, "I am the one and only thing you can count on in this life. I will never leave you nor forsake you. I have laid down my life for you to prove my love for you. No matter what may happen in this life, that is one thing you can count on."

If we anchor our hope for the future in the firm foundation of God's covenant love for us, we can weather any storm life may throw our way. In Jeremiah 29:11, God encourages us to trust and rely on Him, and His plans for us, regardless of what we may be facing. He tell us that His plans are to "prosper you and not to harm you; to give you a hope and a future." Anyone can experience lasting peace, even in the midst of a stormy season of life, by relying on God's covenant love. It's a "with-you-no-matter-what" kind of love.

The rope of hope

I learned a valuable lesson about anchoring to God's covenant love through the most painful experience of my life. I was eighteen and just finishing up fall training camp before my first year of college football at UCLA. In the middle of the night, the dorm room phone rang. It was my mother and her voice shook.

"Tyler, are you awake?" she said. "Are you alert?" From the sound of her voice, I could instantly tell she had called with bad news.

"Yes, Mom, I'm here," I said, instantly alert. "What's going on? Is everything okay?"

"No, honey. I'm so sorry, but I have to tell you something. You're going to be very upset."

My mind raced. What could it be?

"There's been an accident," she said. "A car accident . . . in the city. And it's . . . it's your sister, Aimee. It looks like . . . we're pretty sure . . . Aimee is dead."

My older sister, Aimee, was about to turn twenty-two. Just six months prior, she and Mom had fulfilled a life-long dream, opening a hair salon together near our home.

Mom continued, "Your dad and I need to go to the police department to make sure it is, in fact, Aimee. But they think it's her. When morning comes, I think you should drive home to be here with your family."

So the next morning, I got in my car and began the five-hour drive home. It was the most miserable, tear-filled drive of my life. Along the way, I sobbed so hard I sometimes had trouble catching my breath.

I cried out to God, "Why Aimee? Why now? Why? . . . Why? . . . Why?!"

Our lives—our family—would never be the same. She was so young—how could this happen? How could got have let it happen? Yet, as hurt as I was, I knew I had a choice to make—a choice about how I would respond. Our whole family had a choice to make. As I wrestled with God on the drive home, I prayed—and I think that was the most honest, trusting, hopeful prayer I have ever prayed. It went something like this:

"God, I know You love Aimee, You love me, You love my whole family.

I know your love is real. And I know Aimee's accident is real—*this actually happened*. But there's something I don't get. I don't understand *why* this happened—why You allowed this to happen. It's by far the worst thing that has *ever* happened to us. Worse than when Mom and Dad got divorced. Worse than any injury. Worse than anything.

"So . . . I'm going to try to do something I've never really had to do before—not to this extent. I'm going to *trust* You. At least, I'm gonna try. I'm going to *cling* to You just as if I were swinging out over the ocean—and You're the rope. I'm going to *cling* to You and not let go. Can You keep me from falling? Can You comfort me? And if I lose my grip and fall into the water, will You lower the rope and let me grab onto You? Will You keep me afloat? Will You keep me from sinking? Please, God? Please keep me—and my family—buoyant in the midst of these rough waters. This season of grief and mourning won't last forever, but it's going to be awhile. Please comfort us. Help me—help us—cling to you."

I remember that prayer more vividly than any other prayer I've prayed, almost as if it was yesterday. I remember it more than the prayer I prayed at age twelve, when I asked Jesus to become my Savior and the Lord of my life. I remember it more clearly than the prayers I prayed for God's blessing when I courted Bridget. As long as I live, I'll never forget all the emotions I felt during that drive—the hurt, the spiritual and emotional struggle inside me.

But I also have to tell you this: In the weeks and months that followed the loss of my sister Aimee, God answered my prayer. He answered in big ways and small ways. He was *there*. He was *real*. He was with us. He comforted us. He gave us strength. He kept us afloat, kept us buoyant, kept us aware of His promise to be with us and bless us, to comfort and keep us, to pursue and persist with us, to love and cherish us, to listen and understand us, to be patient and compassionate toward us.

God was my Rock, and the Rock of my family. He proved faithful. He did what only He can do. He turned our mourning into dancing again, just as David wrote in Psalm 30. It didn't happen overnight. In didn't happen as we expected. But He lifted our sorrow and clothed us with joy—right in the middle of our sadness and our utmost pain. It was sweet and savory and inexplicable—but it was *genuine joy*.

God was already my God. But through my sister Aimee's tragic death, while I went through the deep waters that followed, God became my rope of hope for the future. He was my life preserver, my anchor for a future that is firm and secure.

Is God *your* anchor for a firm, secure future? He wants to be. He's waiting for you to turn to Him.

You can trust Him. I know that for a fact, because I learned to trust Him, to trust His covenant love, through one of the most painful experiences I could ever go through. Whatever you're facing, pray that prayer. He'll be with you if you let Him. He'll give you a future that is firm and secured by His covenant love.

Ask Him to be your rope of hope.

QUESTIONS FOR STUDY OR GROUP DISCUSSION

4 | Covenant Relationship—or Consumer Relationship?

1. Do you view your marriage as a covenant relationship or a consumer relationship? Explain your answer. If possible, give examples to support your answer.

2. Describe the most recent situation where you behaved selfishly toward your spouse.

   - What should you have done differently?

   - What can you do now to right that wrong?

3. How good are you at recognizing, admitting, and apologizing for your sins and faults?

   - What makes it hard for you to admit you were wrong and ask forgiveness?

- Do you think your spouse and other family members would think less of you—or more of you—if you were quicker to say, "I was wrong, please forgive me"?

4. In your relationship with God, have you been able to earn God's acceptance? Why or why not?

- Do you worry about whether or not you have done enough to be accepted by God?

- How does your answer to that question affect the way you live?

5
"LOVE *ME!*"

I love Bridget.

In various ways, I try to show her that I genuinely, deeply love her. But I have this problem: I'm a guy. Men and women think and feel differently. Very often, the words and actions I choose as a way of showing my love for Bridget are not really focused on her needs. I am not loving Bridget the way *she* needs to be loved.

Bridget is patient and gentle, and she knows I mean well. I'm grateful that she responds to me in a sensitive way. Here's what she does: She'll give me a hug, and look me in the eyes, and place her hands on either side of my face to get me to focus on her. Then she will say, "Love . . . *ME*."

She's not saying, "Love me." She knows I love her. She's saying, "Love *ME*."

Bridget can tell when I am not truly attentive to her needs. She can tell when I really haven't put much thought into my supposedly "thoughtful" acts of love and service. And when she knows that when I am not really paying attention to *her*, when I'm not being sensitive to *her*, she has to get my full attention and say: "Love *ME*."

She is saying, in effect, "Love me the way I need to be loved." It's easy for me to love her the way *I* want to love her, but real love is loving her the way *she* needs to be loved. This is how we submit to one another in a covenant marriage. Genuine covenant love is not scattershot, it's not generic. It's tightly focused. It's aimed specifically, with pinpoint accuracy, at the target that is your spouse.

How do we love one another with this kind of focused, highly specific love? It takes thought, work, and time. We need to study one another, learn from one another, discover one another, and woo one another. That's right, I said "woo." That's not a word we hear much anymore, but to woo means to court, charm, cultivate a relationship, romantically pursue, and shower with attention and affection.

Paul, in his letter to the Christians at Philippi, describes the attitude of mutual submission as an attitude much like lovers who woo one another. He writes:

> Do nothing out of selfish ambition or vain conceit. Rather, in humility value others above yourselves, not looking to your own interests but each of you to the interests of the others. In your relationships with one another, have the same mindset as Christ Jesus (Philippians 2:3-5).

When lovers woo, they continually value their loved one above themselves, putting the interests of their loved one ahead of their own. That's what covenant marriage should be like—an endless courtship, a continuous wooing of our loved one, a selfless humility and a tireless desire to serve the interests of our marriage partner.

In order to serve your marriage partner, you have to know what his or her needs are. You have to know your marriage partner intimately. You have to be attentive. You have to listen. You have to notice things that are unsaid.

The Scriptures command us to submit to one another in the marriage relationship. This is not an ambiguous command. It specifically means, "Husband, submit to your wife. Wife, submit to your husband." Focus the scope of your attention on one person, get to know the needs of that person, and commit yourself to meeting those specific needs. *You must know someone specifically to love them intimately.*

Submit yourself to the uniqueness and specific needs of your spouse.

Five love languages

The most important book you could ever read about marriage, aside from the Bible, is Gary Chapman's *The Five Love Languages: The Secret to Love That Lasts*. This book has helped save so many marriages that it has remained continuously in print since 1992. You may be thinking, "You want me to read *another* book? I'm barely keeping up in English, and you want me to learn five *love* languages?"

I guarantee that if you learn these five love languages, you'll be very glad you did. And your marriage partner will be even more glad. The five love languages relate to *how* you feel loved by other people—and how your spouse feels loved by you. The five love languages are:

Quality Time
Words of Affirmation
Physical Touch
Gifts
Acts of Service

How do *you* tell your marriage partner, "I love you"?

Perhaps you think the best way to express your love is through words of affirmation. You tell your spouse, "I love you," or, "You mean everything to me," or, "I couldn't live a day without you." You might give compliments to your marriage partner about his or her appearance, or skills and abilities, or sterling character qualities.

But though you lavish words of praise and affirmation on your marriage partner, he or she may still feel unappreciated and unloved. Why? You're speaking the *wrong* language. You can profess your love with all the eloquence of a Shakespeare sonnet, but if your partner's love language is quality time and you are rarely home and you never date your spouse anymore, you are simply wasting your breath.

You may think that the way to say "I love you" is with gifts. But if your spouse's love language is not gifts but acts of service, your partner will say, "Hmph! My spouse thinks I can be bought off with presents and bribes!

What happened to all the thoughtful little acts of service that said 'I love you' when we were dating? That doesn't happen anymore. I just don't feel loved."

There's no point knocking yourself out saying "I love you" in a language your spouse doesn't understand. Instead, take time to find out what his or her love language is—then find multiple ways of saying "I love you" in that language. To do this, you need to study how your marriage partner wants to be loved.

One way to find out is to simply ask: "Honey, what can I do for you that would really say 'I love you'?" The answer may surprise you—and transform your marriage relationship.

Once you know what you're spouse's love language is, you can begin to focus your submission to your spouse in that specific language. You can begin to start meeting your marriage partner's specific and unique needs.

It takes thought to be thoughtful

If you're a guy, brace yourself. I'm about to say something that will rock your world: Your wife's love languages can *change*. That's right. You may know exactly what her love language is today—but tomorrow, or next week, or next year, her love language might be completely different.

Bridget and I did a study together of *The Five Love Languages* when we were first married, and the languages that communicated love to her at that time were Quality Time and Physical Touch. I thought, "Great, I can do that!" And I hard-wired those two love languages into my mind: "I will love and serve Bridget in these two ways. I will submit to her and arrange my life to give her Quality Time and Physical Touch."

I figured I was set for life. As long as I communicated love to her in those two love languages, our relationship would be in great shape.

Then, a couple of years ago, Bridget and I were in a Bible study together. In the course of the study, we talked about the five love languages. "My love languages have changed over time," Bridget said.

I did a double-take. "*What*!?"

"Oh, yeah," she said, "they're different now. Once we started having kids, other love languages became more important to me. Physical Touch is still important—"

"That's my number one love language!" I said. "Let's not get rid of that one!"

"We won't. But Acts of Service are probably number one with me now. We get Quality Time and Physical Touch, and that's fine. But if you did Acts of Service for me that would really meet my specific needs—well, *that* would show me that you *really* love me."

One thing Bridget loves me to do is take out the garbage. And here's the key: Our wives love it if we do our Acts of Service *without being asked*. If she has to ask you to do an Act of Service, it doesn't count for quite as much. Why? Because if you do it without being asked, it shows you're thinking of her wishes and needs. If you have to be asked to do an Act of Service, then you're not communicating in a love language. You're not showing thoughtfulness. You're just doing what's asked of you.

It takes *thought* to be thoughtful. If you aren't thinking of how to be thoughtful to your wife, you aren't communicating "I love you" to your wife.

Learning to communicate in your wife's love language is not as hard as you might think. How hard is it, for example, to take out the trash? It's no big deal to you, but it means so much to her if her love language is Acts of Service. And I'm not just talking about taking the trash cans to the street the night before pickup day. I mean taking out the garbage on a regular basis without being asked. Every evening, just make it a habit to see if the kitchen trash is full, the wastebasket in the bathroom is full, and the other wastebaskets around the house are full. If they are, take them out.

And don't forget to put in a new plastic liner! Don't do half a job.

There's a disparity of perceptions between Bridget and me, and I think this disparity is a very common in marriage: I think I do Acts of Service all the time. Bridget doesn't think I do Acts of Service nearly enough. So, because I don't feel I get enough credit for the Acts of Service I do, I like to point out my Acts of Service to her. In other words— *I like to keep score!*

I don't think Bridget does a good enough job keeping score, so I try to keep score for her. How do I do it? Simple. I don't just take the trash bag quietly out to the trash can. No, I make a production of snapping the empty bag as I'm putting it in the kitchen trash can. Snap, snap, snap! And if Bridget is upstairs, I'll go to the foot of the stairs and snap the bag as loudly as I can.

If she hears all this commotion, she'll ask, "What's all that noise?" And I'll say, "Nothing, honey! I'm just taking out the trash!" I want her to *hear* me emptying the trash, so that she'll know to add one point to my side of the scoreboard.

Another act of service Bridget appreciates is when I take the dishes from the sink and put them in the dishwasher. It's such a simple chore, yet it's surprising how many guys hate to do it. We don't mind getting smeared with grease and motor oil while working on the car. We don't mind playing football in the mud. But ask a guy to scrape food off a dinner plate and put the plate in the dishwasher, and suddenly he doesn't want to get his hands soiled.

Recently, I was on a roll, doing Acts of Service for Bridget. Without being asked, I had taken out the trash. I had mowed the lawns. I had cleaned up my stuff around the house. I had made breakfast and fed the kids. To cap it off, I gathered up the dishes and went to put them in the sink. Then I said to myself, "Hey, Tyler! You're doing great. You're really into this mutual submission thing, you're focused on Bridget and her needs, you're doing Acts of Service. Don't stop there. Don't do half a job."

So, instead of merely stacking the dishes in the sink, I decided to load them in the dishwasher. So I opened the dishwasher and—

Oh, no! The dishwasher was full of *clean* dishes!

Well, you know what *that* means! I was in a classic dilemma. The only way I can put the dirty dishes into the dishwasher was to completely unload all the clean ones! I hadn't counted on that. So there I was, looking into that dishwasher, and I had an angel sitting on one shoulder and the devil on the other.

What did I do? Well, I'm not going to say, because frankly, I don't want to brag.

But I have to confess that, for several long seconds, I looked around in hopes that somebody would be there to observe what I was about to do. I really wanted a witness. More than that, I wanted a scorekeeper. Because this was worth *a lot* of points on the scoreboard!

I'm learning that keeping score, even in small and seemingly insignificant ways like this, is harmful to the marriage relationship. I'm learning that if I truly want to communicate "I love you" to Bridget, then I need to simply do Acts of Service out of love for Bridget, not out of a desire to get points on my scoreboard. Whether she notices and keeps track of my Acts of Service is not nearly as important as the fact that I do them out of a pure and sincere heart of covenant love for Bridget. If I do these acts with the right motivation, if I forget the scoreboard, then over time Bridget will notice, she will be blessed, our marriage relationship will be blessed—

And I will be blessed as well.

The ministry of reconciliation

Most of this chapter has been focused on the practical and personal issues of submitting to one another in marriage. Now let's look at the theological issues.

When there is conflict in a marriage relationship, our natural human tendency is to seek resolution of the issue. But when our focus is on mutual submission instead of our own selfish wants and needs, our higher goal becomes one of reconciliation rather than resolution. When our goal is resolution, we often want to "win," to prove ourselves right and our marriage partner wrong. In other words, we focus on the scoreboard. When conflict comes, we should place a higher value on reconciliation than resolution.

When our higher goal is reconciliation, then the relationship takes priority over the issue. It becomes a matter of covenant love, putting others ahead of self. Our ultimate example is the Lord Jesus Christ Himself. The Scriptures tell us:

> And he died for all, that those who live should no longer live for themselves but for him who died for them and was raised again.
>
> So from now on we regard no one from a worldly point of view. Though we once regarded Christ in this way, we do so no longer. Therefore, if anyone is in Christ, the new creation has come: The old has gone, the new is here! All this is from God, who reconciled us to himself through Christ and gave us the ministry of reconciliation: that God was reconciling the world to himself in Christ, not counting people's sins against them. And he has committed to us the message of reconciliation. We are therefore Christ's ambassadors, as though God were making his appeal through us. We implore you on Christ's behalf: Be reconciled to God (2 Corinthians 5:15-20).

This is a profound revelation! God has given us the ministry of reconciliation—and we are Christ's ambassadors. An ambassador is a person who has been given authority to represent and speak on behalf of a government. So you and I, as Christ's ambassadors, have been given the authority to represent the kingdom of God, and to speak on behalf of King Jesus. God appeals to the world through us. He uses us to show the world what it means to be reconciled to Himself and to one another through acts of mutual submission and reconciliation.

It all starts in the marriage relationship—in your marriage and mine. If we do not exemplify the love, humility, selflessness, and reconciliation of Christ within our own marriages, then what do we have to offer the world? If the Gospel isn't real and powerful in our closest covenant relationships, then how can the Gospel be true anyplace else?

Do you see what a responsibility we have? Do you begin to see the eternal importance of being reconciled to one another, of submitting to one another within the marriage relationship? Do you see how much depends on our obedience in living out covenant love? If we are ambassadors of Christ, representing His kingdom, then our lives and our marriage relationships must reflect the covenant love, forgiveness, and reconciliation He has freely given us.

Learning to communicate in a love language means targeting our marriage partner's greatest need. Jesus modeled this for us perfectly. He communicated with us in our own love language. He targeted our deepest need. What was that need? Our need of *forgiveness*.

In Mark 2, we read the story of Jesus and the paralyzed man. The man's friends took him to a house where Jesus was preaching, but the house was so crowded that they couldn't get the man inside. So they climbed up onto the house and cut a hole in the roof. Then they lowered the paralyzed man down to Jesus on a mat.

When Jesus saw the deep need of the paralyzed man, He spoke—but He didn't say what everyone expected Him to say. He didn't tell the man to rise up and be healed. Instead, Jesus said to the paralyzed man, "Your sins are forgiven."

The people in that house were so shocked that they began to murmur and grumble. Jesus knew what they were thinking, so He said, "Which is easier: to say to this paralyzed man, 'Your sins are forgiven,' or to say, 'Get up, take your mat and walk'? But I want you to know that the Son of Man has authority on earth to forgive sins." So Jesus turned to the man and said, "I tell you, get up, take your mat and go home." And the man was healed.

Jesus focused first on the man's real need, his spiritual need. The paralyzed man needed forgiveness even more than he needed to be able to walk. It's the same with you and me. Our greatest need is spiritual. Your marriage may be paralyzed, and you may want your marriage to be healed—but first God needs to deal with your deepest need, the real issue that paralyzes your marriage.

What is that issue? It's the spiritual issue of sin. It's the core issue of selfishness. You're selfish, your marriage partner is selfish, I'm selfish, my wife is selfish, everybody's selfish. That's just a natural fact.

Most people experience a progression in marriage. There is a courtship that leads to the altar, and after that a honeymoon, followed by some very happy months of newlywed bliss. But time passes, and as you live together in the same house, you begin to find areas of conflict, irritation, and annoyance. You begin to realize how selfish your mate really is! What's worse, your spouse begins to accuse you of being selfish!

If you have good relationship skills, then perhaps you have spent some time talking with your spouse about your differences. Perhaps you even went to a counselor or a pastor to help you with your communication issues and fine-tune your marriage relationship. But as time goes by, usually somewhere in the second or third year of marriage, you begin to think that your marriage partner's selfishness is *much* worse than your own. You struggle with feelings of disillusionment. You want someone to talk to your spouse and say, "Look how wrong and selfish you are!"

In short, you want the Marriage Ref to come to your home, whip out that yellow card or that penalty flag. And if there is no one else handy, you'll appoint yourself as the referee in your marriage.

It's so easy to see our marriage partner's selfishness—and it's so annoying when our partner claims that it's really *we* who are selfish! The problem is that we are unable or unwilling to acknowledge our own selfishness.

What every marriage needs is for both partners to see their own selfishness, to see their need for mutual submission and reconciliation, to see their need for a Savior. But in real life, marriage problems are seldom resolved that neatly. Instead, the finger-pointing, the blaming, the scorekeeping, and the selfishness go on. Neither side sees his or her own selfishness. Neither side will allow the Holy Spirit to melt a stubborn heart, a selfish soul.

If I have just described you and your marriage right now, I want you to know that God's healing power is available to you in your marriage. You can begin to apply the Gospel of Jesus Christ in your own life and in the life of your marriage partner.

That's the number one hope for you and your spouse: to see your mutual need of forgiveness and submission. That's the cure for a marriage that has been paralyzed by selfishness. Even if only one of you sees this right now, you still have the potential for a great marriage.

Be filled with the Spirit

Our need to be healed of selfishness drives us to take a good hard look in the mirror. At first, we think, "I can't look at this. I can't face my own selfishness. I can't accept the fact that I'm to blame for the paralysis in my marriage."

But covenant love forces us to be honest with ourselves, to look unflinchingly in the mirror, and ask ourselves, "What can I do about my own selfishness?" That question drives us to the foot of the cross. It drives us to a place where are able to honestly say, "Lord, I need help. I need grace. I need forgiveness. In our marriage, we need to submit not only to each other, but to you, God, out of gratitude and reverence for Christ."

Why do we have reverence for Christ? Because He recognized our greatest need and He met it. He paid the price. That's the declaration of God who says to us, in effect, "It's okay. Your *sin* is not okay, but I have paid for it through the death of my Son. And because your sin has been paid for, *you* are okay. It cost Jesus the ultimate price, but you are okay when I look at you because of what I have done for you. It's impossible for you to earn it, so just accept it. Now that you are forgiven, use this gift of grace to reach others with the good news of salvation. Be my ambassador. As I have shared this gift with you, go share it with others. As I have loved you, so love one another."

The greatest, deepest, most satisfying and lasting human relationship you can ever have is your marriage relationship—if you have a covenant relationship surrounded and suffused with Christlike covenant love. But to have that kind of marriage relationship, we have to go beyond just forgetting the scoreboard. We have to forgive each other's selfishness over and over again.

You may say, "But Tyler, you don't understand my situation! You don't know what I'm up against! You don't know my spouse!" No, I don't—but I do understand the power of God. I understand it well because I've seen His power change lives and transform marriages. And the key to a transformed marriage is in Ephesians 5:18: "Be filled with the Spirit."

In that passage, Paul commands us to be filled up with the Spirit of God instead of being filled with wine. In marriage, though some people fill themselves with too much wine, more often we are full of selfishness. The key to emptying out your own selfishness, the key to forgiving the selfishness of your spouse, the key to mutually submitting to one another out of reverence for Christ is to be *filled with the Holy Spirit*. How do we do experience the filling of the Holy Spirit? *We ask Him to fill us.*

We pray, "Lord, fill me with Your Spirit. I admit that I am selfish and that I have sinned. I need your forgiveness, I need your grace, I need a Savior. Empty me of all my selfishness, and pour Your Spirit into me. I surrender to Your control. Give me the supernatural power to submit and love and serve my spouse. Reveal to me, day by day and moment by moment, how I can show covenant love to my marriage partner. Lead me, and be my Lord."

That's the prayer of my heart. I believe it's the prayer of your heart, too. It's not a prayer you can pray once and for all. Many of us must renew it daily, even hourly. Yielding to the Spirit of God is the only way to be filled by the Spirit of God—and it's the only way you can bring true health and healing to your marriage.

QUESTIONS FOR STUDY OR GROUP DISCUSSION

5 | "Love ME!"

1. The author uses a word we don't hear very often: "woo." He says it means "to court, charm, cultivate a relationship, romantically pursue, and shower with attention and affection." Do you and your spouse still woo each other?

   - Why or why not?

2. On a scale of 1 to 10, how good a job do you do of focusing on and meeting your spouse's specific needs (1 being the worst, 10 the best)?

   - Based on what your spouse has told you in the past, how do you think your spouse would rate you on that scale?

   - What specific action steps can you take to improve your score?

3. Gary Chapman says there are five love languages that relate to how we feel loved by others. Those five love languages are:

   Quality Time   Gifts
   Words of Affirmation   Acts of Service
   Physical Touch

Have you asked your spouse which of those five love languages are most important to him or her?

- What specific action steps can you take to better meet the love-language needs of your spouse?

4. Which of those five love languages are most important to you? How have you communicated your love-language needs to your spouse?

5. As Christians, we have both a privilege and a responsibility as ambassadors of Christ, as ministers of reconciliation. Are there broken relationships in your life that need to be healed and reconciled?

- What steps can you take this week to live more actively as an ambassador of Christ, as His minister of reconciliation?

6
NAKED AND UNASHAMED

In a marriage, making love is good—but being naked is even better.

Maybe I'd better explain.

Bridget and I were married in Minnesota in August 2001. It was probably the most fun and exciting day of my entire life. It was a party with 200 people attending, and we had a blast. Midwesterners really know how to party. The wedding began at three in the afternoon and Bridget and I didn't leave the reception until after midnight.

The wedding night was everything a wedding night should be.

The following day, we took a cruise on the St. Croix River, which separates Minnesota and Wisconsin, and that night we flew to Hawaii for a twelve-day honeymoon on the Big Island and Maui. It was fantastic!

On our first night in Hawaii, we were both exhausted from the preparations, the wedding day, the emotions, and the long flight to the islands. Now that we were in Hawaii, it was as if all the excitement and adrenaline of the past few days were spent. The roller-coaster ride was over. Now we could relax and begin building a lifetime of memories together.

I remember our first day in Hawaii like it was yesterday. We woke up in the morning and left our room to go for a walk. As I shut the door of our hotel room, I looked at Bridget—and a strange thought hit me. I said, "This may sound totally weird, and I love you more than I can say—but right now, I honestly feel like I barely know you."

"You know what?" she said. "I feel exactly the same way about you."

We went down to the beach, and as we walked along the sand, we talked about those feelings—feelings of love and devotion and romantic bliss, along with the feeling that there was still so much we didn't know about each other.

Now, we were hardly strangers. Bridget and I had dated for a year and a half and we had followed God's leading. We didn't doubt each other's love for a moment. We were sure God had blessed this marriage. We had the support of our friends, family, and pastors. Our marriage was legally recognized, religiously recognized, and had been consummated. We were married in the eyes of the community and in the sight of God, because we celebrated a wedding ceremony and a wedding night.

But we still felt like two people who were deeply intimate yet largely unknown to each other. I hadn't expected that feeling at all. Neither had Bridget.

By contrast, at that same time, I had two best friends, Phil and Tom. I had known each of them ten times as long as I had known Bridget. I knew everything about those guys. I could finish their sentences. I knew all their likes and dislikes, how they ordered their coffee, how they like their steaks cooked, what movies they liked, and on and on.

After knowing Bridget for two years, and dating for a year and a half, I didn't know nearly as much about her. I couldn't finish even one of her sentences. That realization hit me like a ton of bricks.

Now that I'm a pastor and I've done a lot of marriage and pre-marriage counseling, I know that what we felt is not unusual. Young couples come together with a vague expectation that when they marry, they will somehow merge with each other and experience instant intimacy.

I often explain it this way in counseling: We tend to approach marriage as if it were a big box. We think that on our wedding day, we get this box called "Marriage," and inside the box are things like friendship, emotional intimacy, sex, fun, life experiences, children, and on and on. We assume that we will spend our married life together unpacking all the gifts contained inside the marriage box.

But that's not the way it is. In reality, when you get married, you get an *empty* box. And together, over time, you and your mate start filling up your box with the things that make up the marriage. The two of you must fill that box with the friendship, emotional intimacy, and everything else that makes up your marriage relationship.

The reason Bridget and I felt a sense of distance from each other in spite of our love and commitment was simply this: Our box was empty. We were in the first two days of filling up our marriage box, and we had a long way to go. In fact, we are now more than a decade into our marriage and we still have a long way to go. We are still adding new memories, new levels of mutual understanding, and deeper levels of mutual submission to our marriage box.

Today, when I lead a couple through premarital counseling, I draw upon those feelings that Bridget and I experienced on our first full day in Hawaii. I talk to couples about the empty marriage box and about the importance of setting reasonable expectations for the honeymoon, the newlywed years, and beyond.

I should add, just to finish our honeymoon story, that those initial feelings Bridget and I expressed to each other didn't diminish the joy of our honeymoon. In fact, the very act of openly expressing to each other what we were truly feeling was one of the first positive acts we placed in our marriage box. Though that conversation was not physical, it was very intimate. We had our clothes on, yet we were naked. We were building a foundation of honesty and transparency with each other in our marriage that continues to this day.

Naked and unashamed

It was a near-perfect honeymoon. The only reason I say "near-perfect" is because, shortly before we were to return home, we heard the news about the tragic 9/11 attacks. Because air transportation was grounded for the first few days after the terrorist attacks, we were stuck in Hawaii for a few extra days. In spite of bad news from the mainland (plus the fact that our stay in

Hawaii outlasted our funds!), we have beautiful memories of our wedding and honeymoon.

In the process, we learned some important principles about how to build a strong, happy, satisfying marriage that is honoring to God. One of the most important principles we learned is that making love is good—but being naked is better.

Most people think that being naked is part of making love. But I say that making love is part of being naked. Being naked involves being physically open ... and emotionally open ... and intellectually open ... and spiritually open. It involves being open with each other over time. It involves maintaining an attitude of transparency and openness with your marriage partner across all of the experiences of your married life.

We see the importance of being naked in marriage throughout the Scriptures, and especially in the opening pages of the Bible. In Genesis 2, we read about the first married couple in human history:

> The LORD God said, "It is not good for the man to be alone. I will make a helper suitable for him." ... So the LORD God caused the man to fall into a deep sleep; and while he was sleeping, he took one of the man's ribs and then closed up the place with flesh. Then the LORD God made a woman from the rib he had taken out of the man, and he brought her to the man.
>
> The man said,
> "This is now bone of my bones
>   and flesh of my flesh;
> she shall be called 'woman,'
>   for she was taken out of man."
>
> That is why a man leaves his father and mother and is united to his wife, and they become one flesh.
>
> Adam and his wife were both naked, and they felt no shame (Genesis 2:18,21-24).

That is how God made Adam and Eve. God intended that husbands and wives should be naked and unashamed. That is how the first husband and wife were together before sin entered the world. Here we see God's plan for every marriage relationship—that a husband and a wife become one flesh, that they be naked and unashamed. Physical nakedness is only the most superficial form of nakedness—like the outer skin of the onion. There are so many layers of nakedness to be explored and discovered beneath that outermost layer of physical nakedness.

There is intellectual nakedness, in which we reveal to each other our innermost thoughts and goals and dreams. There is emotional nakedness, in which we freely express our feelings, our hurts, our sorrows, our fears, our joys, the things that make us happy and excited, and the emotional needs we tend to keep locked deep inside. There is spiritual nakedness, in which we pray together, worship together, and share our relationship with our Lord, Creator, and Savior.

The goal of marriage is to learn how to be naked and unashamed together in all of these different dimensions of our lives, just as Adam and Eve were before sin entered the world. We are seeking to re-create a little unspoiled Garden of Eden within the marriage relationship.

God's hope for us and our covenant marriage is that we would live in a right relationship with each other and with Him through faith in Jesus Christ. His will is that we would live naked and unashamed before Him and before each other in the marriage relationship—that we would not be dragged down by guilt and emotional burdens, but that we would freely confess our sins, repent of our sin, and celebrate the forgiveness God showers on us through Jesus Christ.

It feels good to be naked in covenant marriage. It's liberating and exhilarating to fully reveal yourself to your life partner, and to plunge into the depths of your partner's mind, soul, and spirit, as well as his or her physical body. But it takes time and thought and intention. Being naked doesn't happen by accident.

On our honeymoon, as Bridget and I thought about how little we really knew about each other, we sensed that something was missing, but we didn't know what it was. Making love is one thing. Being in love is one thing. Being married legally and in the eyes of God is one thing. But there was so much that was missing that we didn't even know about.

Time was missing. Life purpose was missing. Experience was missing. Family was missing. Highs and lows were missing. The day-to-day details of living together were missing. As a married couple, history was missing. All of the little shared marriage moments and shared thoughts were missing. There was so much experiential, intellectual, emotional, and spiritual nakedness we still had to explore before we could truly become as God intended, naked and unashamed.

It's hard for any couple to truly be naked and unashamed with each other. Even after ten, twenty, thirty years or more of marriage, one or both married partners may hold back and remain emotionally withdrawn, intellectually closed, spiritually separate. There are some long-married couples who have never been naked in that sense. They have made love many times—but the idea of showing emotions or becoming spiritually vulnerable is a foreign concept to them.

The Four T's

Bob Turnbull's book *What Your Wife Really Needs* offers profound insights into how husbands can truly be emotionally, relationally, and spiritually naked in the marriage relationship. It all comes down to a very simple concept that Turnbull calls "The Four T's." A wife, he says, needs four things: Time, Talk, Tenderness, and Touch.

Time is the huge issue for women, the first of the Four T's. If you are a husband and you're not in the habit of giving quality time to your wife, then you've got to break your old habits and build a new habit. It's that important. Women want "face time." They want to look you in the eyes and know they have your undivided attention. Guys aren't like that, so they have to consciously work at being aware of their wives' needs.

When guys hang out together, they don't need "face time." They can just be in the general vicinity, hanging out. They don't have to talk, they don't have to be doing anything together. They're just hanging out. This is quality time for guys. "Remember when we hung out?" "Yeah, that was great. Good times."

Women aren't like that. Have you ever seen how two women sit and talk to each other in a coffee shop? They sit across from each other, face-to-face, eye-to-eye, and they lean toward each other. If one of them shares a touching experience or a deep feeling, they reach out, they touch, they connect.

But guys at a coffee shop? They sit at right angles to each other, stretched out, relaxed, no eye contact. They don't talk about feelings. They talk about football, or work, or cars. If two guys go see a movie together, they put an empty seat between them, spread out, no elbows bumping or any other physical touch.

Guys don't need to look at each other or talk to each other. Sometimes, guys will hang out together, and one of them will get up and leave, and it might be ten minutes before the other guy notices his friend is gone. When he finally notices, he thinks, "Oh, he split. Well, we had a good time."

The problem is that many of us as husbands relate to our wives the same way we relate to the guys. We don't *need* face time, so we don't *give* it. But women absolutely need that quality time. When we men don't give our wives what they need, they feel we don't care. As husbands, we need to learn how to give our wives what they need.

Along with time, women need to *talk*, the second of the Four T's. I love what Paul writes in Ephesians 5, where he breaks down the roles of men and women in marriage. He makes one of the most insightful statements in Scripture of how husbands ought to treat wives. After challenging husbands to love their wives as Christ loved the church, he adds that husbands ought to make their wives holy "by the washing with water through the word."

When Paul says "word" here, the original Greek word is *rhema*, which means "speech." He doesn't use the Greek word *logos*, which refers to the Word of God (as when the apostle John wrote, "In the beginning was the Word, and the Word was with God, and the Word was God." The word *logos* can refer to Jesus (the living Word of God), or to the Bible. But *rhema* refers to speech, utterances, or sentences. *Rhema* is talking. So I believe Paul is telling husbands, "If you want a holy and righteous relationship with your wife, talk to her. Bathe her with speech. She loves face time with you, so give her the gift of your quality time."

When you and your marriage partner talk honestly together, you become transparent. You discover that there's so much more to your relationship than making love. You can actually become naked and unashamed through your talk. You explore each other's stories, experiences, highs, lows, sorrows, joys, and feelings. Your wife wants your time, and she wants to talk with you.

And she wants *tenderness*, the third of the Four T's. As the apostle Peter writes, "Husbands, in the same way be considerate as you live with your wives, and treat them with respect as the weaker partner and as heirs with you of the gracious gift of life, so that nothing will hinder your prayers" (1 Peter 3:7). How good are we at showing respect, consideration, and tenderness toward our wives? What steps could we take to show more thoughtfulness and tenderness as husbands?

She also wants *touch*—nonsexual, supportive touch, the fourth of the Four T's. She wants to feel connected to you.

Bridget will often come to me and say, "I'm going through this situation, and I just need you listen, and not give advice, and afterwards I just want a hug," or, "I'm going out and I just want a hug." "Really?" I say. "Okay." And I drop what I'm doing and we hug.

I'm learning that I need to initiate that kind of touch more with Bridget as a way of showing her I love her, I want to be close to her, I want to be connected to her. Honestly, I don't ever remember walking up to Bridget and saying, "Babe, I just need a hug. I just need you to hold me." But she's different than me. I need to take time to be aware of her feelings, to sense those times when she's feeling lonely or vulnerable or uncertain, and she just needs a touch from me to encourage her and help her feel cared for, loved, and embraced. Women need time, talk, tenderness, and touch from their husbands.

The Four C's

Bob Turnbull's wife Yvonne has also written a book. It's called *What Your Husband Really Wants*. In that book, Yvonne suggests that wives should practice what she calls "The Four C's." Yvonne Turnbull has nailed it. These four qualities really speak to what a man wants out of his marriage relationship: He wants a cheerleader, a champion, a companion, and a complement. Let's look at each of these roles:

First, a man wants his wife to be his *cheerleader*. This means you respect him, encourage him, and support him emotionally. You cheer him on.

Randy Pausch was a computer science instructor at Carnegie Mellon University in Pittsburgh, Pennsylvania. When he learned in 2007 that he had terminal pancreatic cancer, and had about six months of good health remaining, he decided to deliver what he called "The Last Lecture: Really Achieving Your Childhood Dreams."

When he told his wife Jai what he wanted to do, she struggled with the idea. In his book *The Last Lecture*, Pausch recalled, "Jai (pronounced 'Jay') had always been my cheerleader. When I was enthusiastic, so was she. But she was leery of this whole last-lecture idea. . . . Jai felt that I ought to be spending my precious time with our kids, or unpacking our new house, rather than devoting my hours to writing the lecture. . . . 'Call me selfish,' Jai told me. 'But I want all of you.' . . . Still, I couldn't let go of my urge to give this last lecture."[1]

Jai's reticence forced Pausch to look honestly at his motivations and ask himself why this last lecture was so important to him. Was he trying to prove that he was strong enough to perform? Was he being a show-off? In a way, the answer was yes to both questions. "An injured lion wants to know if he can still roar," he told his wife. "It's about dignity and self-esteem, which isn't quite the same as vanity."[2] Besides, he had begun to see the lecture as a way to leave a vivid and positive memory of himself to his three young children, ages five, two, and one.

Once Jai knew that he had carefully thought through his motivations, once she saw the last lecture as a gift to their children, she dropped her objections. And once again, she became his cheerleader. The video of Pausch's last lecture went viral on YouTube and became the basis of his best-selling book. Randy Pausch died in July 2008. Even to the final days of his life, he needed his wife to be his cheerleader. And she was.

A man also wants his wife to be his *champion*. What does it mean to be a champion for your husband? It means you praise his strengths and virtues. You defend his reputation. Never attack your husband or criticize him in front of other people. Instead, tell everyone how great he is as a husband, as a father, as a provider, as a spiritual leader. Champion his cause and you will make him *feel* like a champion.

Your husband wants you to be his *companion*. Men may not talk about their feelings, but they've got them. Your husband can face just about anything as long as you are by his side.

My friend and colleague, Pastor Mark Teyler, loves to play golf. One time, Mark was telling me about the vacation he and his wife Tracy had just taken. He told me about the different golf courses he'd played, and I thought, *Wait a minute, he played four rounds of golf during a five-day vacation? That's four or five hours per game!*

I said, "How did you get a free pass from Tracy to play all this golf on your vacation? What was she doing all this time?"

"Oh, Tracy comes with me."

I couldn't believe it! Tracy was in the next room, so I went to her and said, "Tracy! I didn't know you were a golfer!"

"Oh, no," she said. "I don't play golf. I just ride around in the cart with Mark."

"Are you serious?"

"Oh, I love it!" she said. "I bring a book and I enjoy the sunshine and fresh air, and I cheer Mark on."

Now I know why Mark always comes to work singing and wearing a big smile on his face. He's married to a wife who is also his cheerleader and companion.

A husband also wants his wife to be his *complement*. A man wants his wife to complete what he lacks. He's good at some things, she's good at some things, and together they are complete and complementary.

There's a scene in the 1976 movie *Rocky* in which Rocky (Sylvester Stallone) and his friend Paulie (Burt Young) discuss Rocky's girlfriend Adrian (Talia Shire), who happens to be Paulie's sister. Paulie asks, "You like her?"

Rocky says, "Sure, I like her."

"What's the attraction?"

"I dunno . . . she fills gaps."

"What's 'gaps'?"

Rocky shrugs. "I dunno. She's got gaps, I got gaps. Together we fill gaps."

That's what it means for two people to complement each other. They fill gaps. They make up for what is lacking in each other. The strengths of one compensate for the weaknesses of the other.

A man needs a wife who is a cheerleader, a champion, a companion, and a complement to him. A woman needs her husband to give him the gift of time, talk, tenderness, and touch. When a husband and wife demonstrate this kind of thoughtfulness and love in meeting each other's deepest needs, then they can finally become emotionally, intellectually, and spiritually naked with each another. When we know we are loved and forgiven, cherished and respected, known and accepted at a deep and intimate level, we feel safe. The safer we feel, the more freely we can open up to each other and become naked and unashamed.

Making love is good—but being naked is even better.

QUESTIONS FOR STUDY OR GROUP DISCUSSION

6 | Naked and Unashamed

1. On a scale of 1 to 10, how strongly would you agree with this statement: "I feel absolutely free to be emotionally naked with my spouse. I can tell him/her anything and everything about my feelings, my past, and my emotional hurts." (1 = strongly disagree; 10 = strongly agree)

   - If you answered 10, why do you think you feel so emotionally open and free?

   - If you answered less than 10, what holds you back from complete emotional openness and nakedness? Your own feelings? Fear of how your spouse might react? Some other reason?

2. On a scale of 1 to 10, how strongly would you agree with this statement: "I feel absolutely free to be spiritually naked with my spouse. I can tell him/her anything and everything about my daily spiritual experience, my prayer life, my feelings toward God, my spiritual highs and lows, my doubts, my questions." (1 = strongly disagree; 10 = strongly agree)

   - If you answered 10, why do you think you feel so spiritually unrestrained?

- If you answered less than 10, what holds you back from complete spiritual openness and nakedness?

3. What action steps might you take to become more emotionally and spiritually "naked and unashamed" in your marriage?

- How might your spouse be able to help and support you to achieve more openness and "nakedness" in your marriage relationship?

- Bob Turnbull says that wives need "The Four T's," Time, Talk, Tenderness, and Touch. If you are the husband, what specific action steps can you take this week to provide more of what your wife needs?

- Bob Turnbull's wife Yvonne suggests that wives should practice "The Four C's," be a cheerleader, be a champion, be a companion, and be a complement. If you are the wife, what specific action steps can you take this week to provide more of what your husband needs?

7
FROM SELFISHNESS TO SERVANTHOOD

Learn from my faults.

I used to be a husband who over-promised and under-delivered about when I would arrive home. I'd call Bridget and give her an over-optimistic projection of my estimated time of arrival. After disappointing her a number of times, I finally realized that I was only making things worse by arriving home an hour later than I'd promised.

Now I try to under-promise and over-deliver. I'll call home and say, "Honey, I'll be there in an hour and a half or so." Then, if I pull up in the driveway a half-hour earlier than promised and I say "Surprise!" to her and the boys, I can expect a positive response.

I needed to learn not to be selfish. I needed to learn to be more thoughtful and sensitive to Bridget's needs. I'm naturally selfish—and so are you. Don't try to deny it. You *are* selfish. It's part of our human condition.

Selfishness is at the root of all the conflict and division that takes place in marriage. We become enmeshed in conflict, and we don't know how to resolve our conflicts in a godly way. We don't listen, we don't respect out spouse's feelings, we don't ask ourselves, "What if I'm wrong? What if my spouse's complaint about my behavior is valid?" We fight—and we don't know how to forgive, we don't know how to say, "I was wrong. Please forgive me."

And let me say a word at this point to anyone who is not yet married, but may be engaged or in a relationship: Conflict is a good lens through which to examine your relationship. If there's a lot of fighting or bickering between the two of you, take it as a red flag. Don't pretend there is no problem. Don't just hope the problem will go away when you get married. It won't. It will most likely get worse.

Occasional conflict is healthy if you resolve it quickly with mutual forgiveness. A little bit of conflict now and then means that the two of you are confronting your differences honestly and working them out. A relationship in which there is no conflict may be one in which one partner dominates and the other behaves like a doormat—and that's not healthy, either.

On the other hand, if there is frequent and significant conflict in the relationship, conflict that never seems to get resolved, then you'd better get counseling. And when you are in counseling, open your thinking to the possibility that this person may not be God's best for you.

God's goal for your life and mine is that we move from selfishness to servanthood, that we learn the art of forgiving one another. We see this principle illustrated for us in an Old Testament book, The Song of Solomon.

Two selfish people

One of the shortest books in the Bible, The Song of Solomon is a romantic poem about King Solomon and his bride, who is identified only as "the Shulamite." It is a story of their courtship, marriage, and the consummation of their marriage in the bridal chamber. Their lovemaking is presented beautifully and lyrically, depicting married sexual expression as God intended.

Though the Song of Solomon is often interpreted as an allegorical representation of God's relationship with Israel or with His Church, it should also be taken literally as a powerful and practical reflection of God's plan for covenant marriage. One of the principles that becomes clear in this beautiful book is that, even after the king and his bride have made love together, they don't yet know how to be "naked and unashamed" with each other.

Their sexual intimacy is described in poetic metaphors. The bride speaks:

> Awake, north wind,
>   and come, south wind!
> Blow on my garden,

that its fragrance may spread everywhere.
Let my beloved come into his garden
   and taste its choice fruits (Song of Solomon 4:16).

When Solomon responds, it becomes clear that their marriage has been consummated. Solomon says:

I have come into my garden, my sister, my bride;
  I have gathered my myrrh with my spice.
I have eaten my honeycomb and my honey;
  I have drunk my wine and my milk
(Song of Solomon 5:1a).

The figurative language veils what has taken place: The sweet, spicy myrrh he has gathered, the honey he has eaten, the wine and milk he has drunk—all of these images refer to the pleasures of the king's sexual experience with his wife.

Then come two lines that many Bible scholars think are actually spoken by God, a kind of divine commentary on the blessedness of sexual expression within marriage:

Eat, friends, and drink;
  drink your fill of love (Song of Solomon 5:1b).

In other words, God is saying to this newlywed couple, "Be naked and unashamed! Enjoy the sweet pleasures of married love!"

But then something goes wrong for this newlywed couple. Though they clearly know how to make love, the king and his bride still need to learn how to be naked and unashamed as God intends us to be in covenant marriage. The bride says:

I slept but my heart was awake.
  Listen! My beloved is knocking:
"Open to me, my sister, my darling,

>   my dove, my flawless one.
> My head is drenched with dew,
>   my hair with the dampness of the night"
> (Song of Solomon 5:2).

She has probably been waiting for her lover to return home to her. It's late, and she is dozing off. She sleeps lightly—yet her heart is still awake. Then she hears her lover's knock at the door of her bedchamber. He calls to her, using every term of endearment he can think of—"my sister, my darling, my dove, my flawless one."

He also says that his head is drenched with dew. Why would his head be so damp because of the night? It's because he's coming home from a long day's work. He is King Solomon, and he has a kingdom to run. He probably wanted to cut his work short and rush home to his bride, but the chores of chairing an earthly kingdom kept him away from her for hours. Now he arrives late at night and knocks on her bedroom door.

At this point, I have to mention one aspect of the story that I have a hard time wrapping my mind around—the fact that King Solomon and his bride sleep in separate bedrooms. Maybe that was just the accepted practice of ancient kings. Perhaps they reasoned that, since they had an opulent palace to live in, why shouldn't the king and his bride have their own bedrooms? Well, I think it's an absurd arrangement, and I'm sure you do as well, but that's the situation we see here in the Song of Solomon.

The king comes to the bedroom of his bride and knocks at her door. It's obvious what's on his mind. "Open to me, my sister, my darling, my dove, my flawless one," he says. But how does she respond? She replies:

> I have taken off my robe—
>   must I put it on again?
> I have washed my feet—
>   must I soil them again? (Song of Solomon 5:3).

She turned him down! It's the equivalent of, "Not tonight, dear. I just washed my hair." This is an impasse that is familiar to every married couple. He's willing, he's ready—but she's not. She might have been ready for love an hour or two ago, but he came home too late! She's probably the only person in the kingdom who can say "no" to the king without being sent to the dungeon.

Why did the king's bride reject him? Most biblical scholars think she was punishing him for some reason. Perhaps she felt that, by staying out and working late, he was ignoring her. She wanted him home early—and maybe he even *promised* to be home early—but when he didn't arrive according to her expectations, she went into a pout. She withheld sex from him. This was a selfish response on her part.

But let's be fair. A persuasive case can be made that there was selfishness on the king's part as well. He arrived home late and expected his bride to be instantly available to him. He wasn't thinking about her needs and feelings. So if you are a husband, learn from King Solomon's mistakes.

Here in this passage, we see two people who have behaved selfishly. Their mutual selfishness has created a barrier in their relationship.

Myrrh on the door-latch

The impasse between the king and his bride is something every married couple has experienced. What happens next?

> My beloved thrust his hand through the latch-opening;
> my heart began to pound for him (Song of Solomon 5:4).

In an instant, when the king reaches through an opening to touch the door-latch, something changes within his bride. The mere fact that he wants to come in and be with her awakens the desire within her.

> I arose to open for my beloved,
> and my hands dripped with myrrh,
> my fingers with flowing myrrh,

on the handles of the bolt.
I opened for my beloved,
   but my beloved had left; he was gone.
My heart sank at his departure (Song of Solomon 5:5-6a).

Notice this fascinating detail: There is myrrh on the door-latch. What does that mean? Myrrh is a fragrant spice derived by cutting a wound into the bark of the balsam poplar tree, also known as the balm of Gilead tree. The wound causes the tree to bleed from its sapwood, and the fragrant balm, the myrrh, is collected and used in making the royal perfume. The ancients sometimes prized myrrh more highly than gold. Along with gold and frankincense, it was one of the three gifts presented to the baby Jesus by the wise men from the East (see Matthew 2:11).

Why was there myrrh on the door-latch? Because there was myrrh on the king's hand when he touched the latch. He had prepared himself for a night of lovemaking by dipping his hands in fragrant myrrh, the royal perfume. Perhaps he had planned to begin by giving her a fragrant body massage, combining lovemaking with aromatherapy. He had placed his myrrh-dripping fingers on the door-latch—but her unexpected refusal had stopped him from opening the door.

So when the bride touched the latch then took her hand away, her fingers were fragrant with myrrh. In an instant, she pictured her beloved preparing himself for lovemaking, applying the myrrh to make himself more pleasing to her. That touch of spice revealed her beloved's heart. In a flash, she realized all the love and desire he had for her—and she regretted her selfish rejection of his love. "I opened for my beloved," she said, "but my beloved had left; he was gone. My heart sank at his departure."

Why did he leave? He'd been so close to opening the door—but then he abruptly turned and walked away. Perhaps he was surprised and hurt that his bride had latched the door against him. She had never refused him before. But he didn't try to force his way in. He didn't raise his voice.

I love the king's wisdom in choosing not to fight with his bride. If you're a husband, consider King Solomon's wise example. Don't fight with your wife. Even if you win, you lose! Instead of fighting, Solomon takes a time out and goes away to cool off.

Notice that when the bride realized that her beloved had gone, her heart sank! She had chased him away with her selfishness. In fact, the king and his bride had hurt each other with their *mutual* selfishness. He was selfish with the management of his time. She was selfish with the management of their sexual experience. This example is just as common among marriages today, and serves as a great example of the timeless truth of the Bible.

As the apostle Paul writes in 1 Corinthians, "The wife does not have authority over her own body but yields it to her husband. In the same way, the husband does not have authority over his own body but yields it to his wife. Do not deprive each other . . ." (1 Corinthians 7:4-5). Paul adds that Christian couples should not deprive each other of sex except by *mutual* agreement, so that they can devote themselves to prayer for a period of time—a kind of "fasting" from sex. If you and your marriage partner fast from sex for spiritual reasons, that's good—but once the fast is ended, *break that fast*.

It's clear in God's Word how Christian husbands and wives are to relate to each other and treat each other in their sexual relationship. But we are selfish. And our selfishness keeps us from becoming what God intended us to be as husbands and wives. Selfish people make terrible lovers, terrible spouses, and terrible parents. Selfish people leave terrible legacies.

A path to reconciliation

The king had departed. His bride didn't know where he'd gone. So she went looking for him, calling for him, wanting him—but she couldn't find him anywhere. This scene, in which the bride searches for her departed husband, parallels a scene in Song of Solomon 3, in which she experiences a nightmare of abandonment:

> All night long on my bed
> > I looked for the one my heart loves;
> > I looked for him but did not find him (Song of Solomon 3:1).

After that nightmare, she goes out into the city, looking for her beloved—and she cannot find him. Instead, she encounters the watchmen as they make their rounds of the city. She asks them if they have seen the king. Before they can answer, she sees her beloved and runs to him. All of this takes place in chapter 3.

But here, in Song of Solomon 5, her worst nightmare has come true. It's not just a dream. Her husband really has departed from her. She is panicked and afraid because she has sent him away—and she doesn't know where to find him. She says:

> I looked for him but did not find him.
> > I called him but he did not answer.
> The watchmen found me
> > as they made their rounds in the city.
> They beat me, they bruised me;
> > they took away my cloak,
> > those watchmen of the walls! (Song of Solomon 5:6b-7)

It's dark. The watchmen find her—but they don't recognize her. They don't know she is the bride of the king. When they see her running through the streets, calling for her beloved, they think she is an immoral woman. They stop her, beat her, and strip her clothes from her. But all she can think of is finding the husband she sent away. She says:

> Daughters of Jerusalem, I charge you—
> > if you find my beloved,
> > what will you tell him?

Tell him I am faint with love (Song of Solomon 5:8).

Then she experiences a flash of insight—and she knows exactly where her beloved has gone. She says:

> My beloved has gone down to his garden,
>   to the beds of spices,
> to browse in the gardens
>   and to gather lilies.
> I am my beloved's and my beloved is mine;
>   he browses among the lilies (Song of Solomon 6:2-3).

Some Bible scholars believe that these references to "beds of spices" and browsing and gathering lilies "in the gardens" may be veiled references to a harem or seraglio, a place where women attendants or concubines are gathered. She tells herself that she will go there and win him back, because "I am my beloved's and my beloved is mine."

What made her think that he might have gone to the "beds of spices"? Perhaps it was the fragrance of rich, spicy myrrh that had dripped from the king's fingers onto the door-latch. Myrrh was a strong symbol of their love. That fragrance had been part of their love-making. It was how they showed affection to each other. That scent communicated, far more powerfully than words, "I'm here, I'm available to you, I love you with all my heart and soul."

I believe the myrrh on the door-latch was no accident. I think the king deliberately dripped myrrh on the latch as a reminder of their love. Why would he do that? He did it to give her a path back to him.

The myrrh on the door-latch was the king's way of saying, "I'm not happy with your rejection. I understand that you want to punish me for coming home late, but you've hurt me. So I'm going—and I'm leaving you this fragrant reminder of our love, of what we mean to each other. I'm giving you a path back to me. If you think about it, you know where to find me. I'll be waiting." He didn't say that in words. He didn't need to. The myrrh on the door-latch said it all.

You and your marriage partner may have a symbol like this—some token that provides a path back after a time of conflict. It might be a gift of flowers. It might be an act of service. It might be a special dinner. It is a tangible way of saying, "My love for you is greater than this momentary conflict. I want to reconcile with you. I want to forgive and be forgiven."

The scent of myrrh reminds the bride of all that her beloved means to her, of all the love and affection they've shared together. So she pursues him. He has initiated reconciliation by not escalating the conflict, by leaving the myrrh on the door-latch, and by leaving a pathway back. She initiates by taking that path, by pursuing her beloved, even at the risk of being abused by the watchmen.

When you and your marriage partner are in conflict, do you do that? Do you give him or her a path back? Do you pursue your mate? Do you initiate reconciliation? Or do you block the path and slam the door to reconciliation? Do you and your mate punish each other and prolong the conflict?

The bride finds her beloved in the garden, and they come face-to-face. What happens next? Does the king demand an apology? Does he berate her for rejecting him? Does he say, "You were totally wrong! You're supposed to submit to me! Not only am I your husband, but I'm the king! You're supposed to do what I say! You're never supposed to deprive me!"

Does she scold him for staying out too long, then expecting to have sex so late at night? Does she say, "You were wrong! Here we are, two newlyweds, yet you think you can come and go as you please, make love whenever it's convenient for you, and never give a thought to my feelings! So you're the king! Would it hurt you to show a little consideration, a little thoughtfulness?"

No, none of that happens. Instead, they embrace—and they quickly move from fighting to forgiving, from selfishness to serving one another. The king says:

> You are as beautiful as Tirzah, my darling,
>   as lovely as Jerusalem,
>   as majestic as troops with banners.
> Turn your eyes from me;
>   they overwhelm me.
> Your hair is like a flock of goats
>   descending from Gilead (Song of Solomon 6:4-5).

And he goes on to speak adoringly of her charm and her beauty, calling her "my dove, my perfect one." When he compares her to Tirzah and Jerusalem, he chooses the two most beautiful cities in the world, known for their lush gardens and sparkling reflecting pools. He compares her to the majesty of a mighty army that flows over hills under rippling silken banners.

What is he doing? He's doing what the apostle Paul said in Ephesians 5: He is making his bride holy by washing her with words. He forgives her, and she forgives him. Here is a beautiful example for you and me: Always be quick to forgive. Always be quick to serve. Always be quick to use words that heal.

Our role model

We are selfish people, and we naturally want to be served rather than to serve. God wants to move us from selfishness to servanthood. But how do we do that?

Mutual forgiveness in marriage is only made possible through the forgiveness Jesus Himself brings through His death and resurrection. His forgiveness is the pattern for our forgiveness.

A pastor once gave his congregation this challenge: "Ask your wife or your husband, 'On a scale of one to ten, how selfish am I?' Then listen for the answer. Don't argue with the answer, don't defend yourself. Just receive the answer and think about it. Then ask this follow-up question: 'What can I do to serve you better?'"

If you *really* want a reality check, go to your friends as well—people you can trust to tell you the truth, who won't just tell you what you want to hear. Ask: "On a scale of one to ten, how selfish do you think I am? What can I do to become a better servant?"

I have done this exercise, and I have learned a lot about myself that I didn't know before. I have learned that I am not as good a servant as I thought I was. I am more selfish than I realized. And I have learned what I can do—what I *must* do—in order to change, to move from selfishness to servanthood.

I once visited Jerusalem with Pastor Mark Campbell, a friend and fellow staffer at Neighborhood Church. During one of our last days in Israel, we ventured out into the old city. It was raining and we were caught in a narrow street where the rain washed down and there was no shelter from the downpour. We had no umbrellas, and we hurried along, looking for a doorway to duck into. The first place we found was a little shop that sold old photographs. Once inside, we talked to the owner and learned that he was a photographer whose father and grandfather had also been professional photographers.

"Shortly before my father died," he told us, "my wife said we should clean out my father's attic. We discovered thousands of old pictures that my father and grandfather had taken of old Jerusalem, and all around Israel." So he had built a thriving business selling prints of those fascinating images of a bygone Israel.

I looked around the store and I was captivated by one picture of a shepherd with his sheep, sitting on the Mount of Olives, looking over the old city. The photo had been taken about 75 years ago, before much of the urbanization that exists today. I bought the photo, had it framed, and I now have it hanging in my office. It reminds me every day that, as a pastor, I am not a boss. I'm a shepherd. I'm a servant. My job is to serve the needs of my sheep.

In my marriage, God calls me to be a leader, just as Jesus is the leader of the church. How did Jesus lead? By serving. As Jesus told His disciples, "If anyone wants to be first, he must be the very last, and the servant of all" (Mark 9:35). So, in our marriages, husbands are called to be not just leaders, but *servant*-leaders. As Paul wrote to the church in Philippi:

> Do nothing out of selfish ambition or vain conceit. Rather, in humility value others above yourselves, not looking to your own interests but each of you to the interests of the others.
>
> In your relationships with one another, have the same mindset as Christ Jesus: Who, being in very nature God, did not consider equality with God something to be used to his own advantage; rather, he made himself nothing by taking the very nature of a servant, being made in human likeness.
>
> And being found in appearance as a man, he humbled himself by becoming obedient to death—even death on a cross! (Philippians 2:3-8).

Jesus the Servant is our role model. As He told His disciples, "the Son of Man did not come to be served, but to serve, and to give his life as a ransom for many" (Matthew 20:28). The first shall be last. The greatest is the least. The way up is down.

QUESTIONS FOR STUDY OR GROUP DISCUSSION

7 | From Selfishness to Servanthood

1. Every marriage experiences conflict from time to time. Would you say that you and your spouse resolve conflict in a healthy, constructive way or an unhealthy, destructive way?

2. What is one thing you tend to do or say that causes unhealthy conflict in your relationship?

   - What specific action steps could you take to change your behavior and become less selfish and more constructive in times of conflict?

3. Think back to the last fight you had with your spouse. Looking back, what one thing could you have done differently to defuse the situation?

   - Why didn't you choose to do that? Was selfishness a factor in your side of the argument?

   - Again, thinking back to your last fight with your spouse, did you close the door to reconciliation—or did you leave your spouse a path back to you?

4. The author writes that the path back, the "myrrh on the door-latch" in your relationship, might be "a gift of flowers. It might be an act of service. It might be a special dinner. It is a tangible way of saying, 'My love for you is greater than this momentary conflict. I want to reconcile with you. I want to forgive and I want to be forgiven.'"

- What is one thing you could do in times of conflict to give your spouse a path back? In other words, what would be your "myrrh on the door-latch"?

5. If you dare, take the challenge suggested in this chapter: Ask your wife or husband, "On a scale of one to ten, how selfish am I?" Don't argue or defend yourself—just listen to the answer and think about it. Then ask: "What can I do to serve you better?"

- Consider asking the same question of your trusted friends: "On a scale of one to ten, how selfish do you think I am? What can I do to become a better servant?"

- What specific actions can you take to implement that feedback in your relationships, and especially in your marriage?

8
HEAR THE CALL

In the summer of 1963, a legislator gave a speech to a men's-only civic club. In the course of his speech, he complained about a women's organization, the American Association of University Women, which was highly critical of his political views. "We don't have any of these university women in Perry County," the politician said, "but I'll tell you what we do up there when one of our women starts poking around in something she doesn't know anything about: We get her an extra milk cow. If that don't work, we give her a little more garden to attend to. And then if that's not enough, we get her pregnant and keep her barefoot."

The legislator's remarks were published in the local newspaper. At the very next election, the women voters of his district went to the polls, proudly removed their shoes as a show of defiance, stepped barefoot into the voting booth, and cast their votes to send him into retirement.[1] And deservedly so.

Ever since that time, the expression "keep her barefoot and pregnant" has been a symbol of male oppression of women. The idea is that if a man keeps his wife pregnant, year after year, she'll never have time to get out of the house and she won't need any shoes.

Unfortunately, many people miss the point of the apostle Paul's teaching on marriage in his letter to the Ephesians. They read what the apostle writes about submission, and they think, "Oh, that is so old school! That's just an old male chauvinist spouting his male dominance propaganda. Paul is practically saying, 'Men, you've gotta keep your wives barefoot and pregnant!'"

But that's not what the apostle Paul is saying.

We've already spent some time camped out on the opening verse of Paul's teaching on marriage, Ephesians 5:21—"Submit to one another out of reverence for Christ." We've looked at that verse from several different angles and summed up the meaning of that verse in one statement: "Forget the scoreboard." If you want a healthy, godly, satisfying marriage relationship, stop keeping score. Instead, arrange your attitudes, interests, and actions to place them under submission to your marriage partner. In the ultimate section of Scripture on marriage, this is God's all-encompassing command. We listen to Him because he's The Marriage Ref, the One who created the covenant of marriage. We listen to Him because He loves us. And if we follow His guidelines, good things will happen in our marriage.

Now we come to the rest of the Paul's teaching, Ephesians 5:22-33. This is the Big Daddy passage on marriage—and I have to be honest: I approach this passage with my knees knocking. Why? Because the teaching in this passage is nitty and it's gritty, and it's a bit gnarly. You may not like everything you read and hear.

So as we begin working our way through Paul's teaching about marriage, I have one big question for you: Do you believe God is good?

I'll assume you answered, "Yes!"

Now, if we believe God is good, then what does that mean for your life and mine? It means that God is *for* us. So if God is good and God is for us, then the teaching He gives us in His Word must be good for our lives.

And here in Ephesians 5, God gives us a passage that contains His essential guidelines for how to live together as husband and wife. And if God is good and He is for us, then if we follow His guidelines, we will be blessed. Do you believe that?

We're about to plunge into one of the most challenging, most unpopular passages in all of Scripture. Paul's teaching in Ephesians is especially scorned by our secular culture. This passage of Scripture will test us to our core. But these verses contain God's game plan for covenant marriage. If we follow this plan in our own marriages, if we allow the Holy Spirit to be not just our Marriage Ref but our Coach as well, then we will experience transformation in our marriage relationships.

Right here, in Ephesians 5, God draws the Xs and Os of His game plan for marriage. This is His chalk talk. This is where he gives us the plays and assignments that will bring us success and satisfaction. Because God is good, because He is for us and He is our coach, we can trust Him—and we can trust the pattern of marriage that He lays out for us in His Word.

In this chapter, and in the two chapters to follow, I'm going to frame the teaching of Ephesians 5 in three ways:

1. We need to *hear the call*. God wants us to hear His call to husbands and wives.
2. We need to *understand the Fall*. The Fall of humanity in Genesis 3 explains why it is so hard for us to hear and heed the call. We'll explore this insight in Chapter 9.
3. We need to *hold the ball*. This is a football analogy. One of the first skills you learn in football is "ball security," holding the ball in such a way that you don't fumble the ball away. Similarly, one of the most important skills in marriage is protecting and securing your marriage so that you don't fumble your marriage relationship away. We'll explore this analogy further in Chapter 10.

First, let's learn how to hear the call.

Wife, hear the call

Paul states his over-arching theme for this passage in Ephesians 5:21—"Submit to one another out of reverence for Christ." Then he goes on to explore the many facets of mutual submission in marriage:

> Wives, submit yourselves to your own husbands as you do to the Lord. For the husband is the head of the wife as Christ is the head of the church, his body, of which he is the Savior. Now as the

church submits to Christ, so also wives should submit to their husbands in everything.

Husbands, love your wives, just as Christ loved the church and gave himself up for her to make her holy, cleansing her by the washing with water through the word, and to present her to himself as a radiant church, without stain or wrinkle or any other blemish, but holy and blameless. In this same way, husbands ought to love their wives as their own bodies. He who loves his wife loves himself. After all, no one ever hated their own body, but they feed and care for their body, just as Christ does the church—for we are members of his body. "For this reason a man will leave his father and mother and be united to his wife, and the two will become one flesh." This is a profound mystery—but I am talking about Christ and the church. However, each one of you also must love his wife as he loves himself, and the wife must respect her husband (Ephesians 5:21-33).

Whether you are a husband or a wife, it takes a soft, humble heart to receive this teaching from God. It takes courage to squarely face the conviction in these verses. Living out Paul's instructions for a godly marriage goes against human nature—and it saws across the grain of our prideful, self-centered culture. So we need to ask the Holy Spirit to teach us and move in power within us.

Do you hear the call in these verses? Paul writes, "Wives, submit yourselves to your own husbands as you do to the Lord. For the husband is the head of the wife as Christ is the head of the church, his body, of which he is the Savior. Now as the church submits to Christ, so also wives should submit to their husbands in everything." When I bring up these verses in my teaching on Christian marriage, or during a premarital counseling session with a couple, I can see the barriers go up on women's faces. This is clearly *not* a very popular teaching among wives.

Occasionally, some foolhardy husband will call out, "Preach it, brother!" And I think, "There's one guy who'll be sleeping on the couch tonight."

But God has issued a call to us in these verses. Paul's letter to the Ephesians is God's Word. We have agreed that God is good, and that this passage contains God's plan for marriage. And obedience to God's plan leads us to blessing. So you and I have to honestly wrestle with what God is saying to us through His servant Paul.

"Wives, submit yourselves to your own husbands. . . . Wives should submit to their husbands in everything." Obviously, that's an error in translation, right? No, the translation is sound. This passage says what it says, and what it says is what it says.

Many wives, upon encountering this passage, say, "Okay, I can submit . . . as long as I agree with what I'm submitting to." That's like saying, "I'm willing to submit to the traffic laws as long as I agree with them." Or, "I always submit to the laws against shoplifting—unless, of course, I see a $5,000 Gucci handbag that I just *have* to have." When you only submit to what you agree with, it's not really submission. It's just doing what you want to do.

Genuine submission means you willingly submit even when you *don't* agree. You voluntarily submit even when it's not easy and not pleasant.

Submission is not some strange concept Paul invented in his letter to the Ephesians. This passage is in full agreement with all biblical teaching on what it means to be a godly wife. Read Titus 2, 1 Corinthians 11, Colossians 2, or 1 Peter 3. The same commands you find here in Ephesians 5 are found in each of those passages.

And husband, it's important that you understand that your wife's submission is not something you can command. God can (and does) command it, but you cannot. Nowhere in Scripture does it say that you are to force or browbeat your wife into submission. This passage is directed at wives, and it commands the wife to willingly, lovingly, voluntarily submit to her husband as unto the Lord.

Husband, hear the call

As a pastor, my job involves getting up in front of the people, opening the Scriptures, and teaching the Word of God. And when I teach from God's Word, I often need to "raise the tension." In other words, I often need to find a way to make the meaning of Scripture so clear that my hearers cannot escape its meaning, cannot rationalize it away, cannot say to themselves, "This verse applies to my neighbor. It doesn't apply to me." That's what it means to get people to wrestle honestly with what the Scriptures say.

But here in Ephesians 5, I don't have to raise the tension at all. I don't have to underscore or illustrate or emphasize to raise the tension of this passage. The tension is here, it's real, it's palpable, it's inescapable. When I stand up and teach from Ephesians 5, I can feel the tension in the air, and I can see it in the faces looking back at me.

So we have to acknowledge the tension in this passage. We have to acknowledge that it says what it says, and what it says is what it says. Wives have to wrestle with the call of God and His Word on their lives—and so do husbands. And God's call to husbands is every bit as challenging and demanding as His call to wives.

Now, husband, hear the call of God in His Word: "Husbands, love your wives, just as Christ loved the church and gave himself up for her." It says what it says, and what it says is not sexist, not chauvinist. God has raised the bar incredibly high for husbands. The Christian husband is to show himself to *be like Christ*. Remember what Paul wrote to the Christians in Philippi:

> Do nothing out of selfish ambition or vain conceit. Rather, in humility value others above yourselves, not looking to your own interests but each of you to the interests of the others. In your relationships with one another, have the same mindset as Christ Jesus (Philippians 2:3-5).

Our attitude should be the attitude of Jesus Himself. He loved the church and gave His life for the church—and God calls you, husband, to do the same for your wife. He calls you to love her as Christ loved the church. As Paul goes on to say, Jesus "made himself nothing by taking the very nature of a servant" (Philippians 2:7). He emptied Himself, made Himself nothing for the sake of His bride, the church. And He is our example: God calls you, husband, to empty yourself, to make yourself nothing, to take the form of a servant for the sake of your bride.

In short, when your wife thinks of you, she should think of Jesus Christ. She should see His life living in you. If you are a husband, that is God's call upon your life.

And it's a challenging call, isn't it? No one who truly understands that call can say that the apostle Paul, writing in Ephesians 5, is a sexist or a chauvinist. "Wives, submit yourselves to your own husbands," Paul writes—but then he goes on to say, in effect, "Husbands, be servants to your wives. Be humble and Christlike. Empty yourself and pour yourself out for your bride. Lay down your life for her." No sexist or chauvinist could issue such a call—nor obey such a call.

Husband, are you wrestling honestly with the call of God upon your life and your marriage? Your wife is asking herself, "Jesus pursues me always; does my husband? Jesus loves me always; does my husband? Jesus forgives me always; does my husband? Jesus is merciful to me always; is my husband? Jesus is always tender with me and He always gives me the word that I need; does my husband? Jesus always has grace for me; does my husband? Jesus gave up His life for me; does my husband?"

As the husband, you are the Christ-figure in your covenant marriage! When your wife thinks of you, she should think of Jesus Christ. She should see His life reflected in your words and actions. Husband, hear the call and obey it—and your entire family will be blessed.

There's no quid pro quo

In Christian marriage, covenant marriage, God issues a call to wives and a call to husbands. These calls are different, yet reciprocal and mutual. Both the husband and wife are called to submit, but his submission takes a different form from hers.

The world looks at this teaching and says, "This is all wrong! Women should never submit to a man! Stand up for your rights, ladies! Demand your equality!" Yet the worldly view often misses the beautiful symmetry in God's call to mutual submission.

The worldly male view says, "Don't let any woman lead you around by the nose! Show her who's boss! Be a man!" The worldly view cannot see how true manhood is fully expressed through being a servant to your wife, through pouring yourself out for her and sacrificing yourself for her. There is no greater example of authentic manhood than Jesus Christ, the Servant of His bride, the church.

True equality between man and wife is found in God's plan of mutual submission. Wife, as you submit to your husband, your husband is called to submit to the Lord of the Universe—and he is accountable to his Lord for the way he serves you in the marriage. Husband, God calls you and holds you accountable to present your wife to Him as a radiant bride "without stain or wrinkle or any other blemish, but holy and blameless." He calls you to love her as you love your own body. This is a serious responsibility.

What would it look like if you, husband, truly loved your wife as Christ loved the church and gave himself for it? What would your side of mutual submission look like?

Look, I know that men don't exactly like to read "relationship books." So, husband, before I go on to give you some suggestions, I'd like to make sure I have your attention (ladies, excuse me for shouting), so—

HUSBAND, LISTEN UP!

I'm going to make this *really easy* for you. I'm going to bullet-point some ways that you can demonstrate Christlike submission and love for toward your wife. You can scoop up these ideas and implement them today:

- *Be the leader*. As a Christian husband, become the spiritual leader in your home. Initiate prayer and Bible study with your wife and children. Initiate involvement in a small group Bible study in your church.
- *Show you care*. Show your wife that you genuinely care about her feelings and needs. Ask her about her day and about the things she truly cares about. Listen to her with complete, undivided attention. Speak positively and affirmingly, both *to* you wife and *about* her to others.
- *Be a servant*. Serve your wife in an active and pro-active way. Don't wait for her to ask you for your help. Take out the garbage, wash the dishes, pick up your clothes, help her make the bed, offer to do the vacuuming and other back-bending chores around the house. Astonish her with your eagerness to serve her as Christ served the church.
- *Seek her opinions*. Show that you respect her thoughts and feelings. Pray for her every day—and tell her you pray for her. Give her thoughtful gifts and leave thoughtful notes for her. Let her know that she is always in your thoughts and prayers.
- *Initiate peacemaking*. Become a loving, forgiving peacemaker in your home. When there is conflict, respond to her gently and calmly. Make a commitment to never respond to her with shouting, sarcastic words, or a condescending tone of voice. If she has a complaint about your words or behavior, drop your defenses. Be willing to consider her feelings and admit that you were wrong.
- *Initiate relationship improvement*. Look for opportunities to improve your marriage relationship by attending couples conferences and Christian marriage seminars. Plan romantic getaways. Have a regular weekly "date night" with your wife.

Give your wife the gift of your time and affection.
- ***Facilitate family worship.*** Take responsibility for getting up early on Sunday mornings, helping to get the children dressed and fed, and making sure the family leaves on time to get to church with a stress-free, worshipful attitude.

These are just a few suggestions. I'm sure you can think of other acts of service you can do to submit yourself to your wife and *become the initiator* in meeting her deepest needs. I guarantee, if you truly become the kind of husband Paul describes in Ephesians 5, she will eagerly become the kind of wife Paul describes. What Christian wife wouldn't feel honored and blessed to have a husband like that?

Before I close out this chapter, a word to you, the wife (husband, feel free to tune out for the next two or three paragraphs).

Wife, let me ask you this: What are you doing to enable your husband to willingly, eagerly answer that call? Please don't nag him or rub his nose in Ephesians 5. That's not answering God's call to you to submit to your husband. Don't try to make your husband *earn* your submission. Please understand: God's command for you to submit to your husband is not based *at all* on his merit. It's based *entirely* on your own reverence for Jesus Christ as Lord of your life. God's call upon you is that you submit to him, freely and voluntarily.

You don't *trade* submission, as if it were a quid pro quo. You don't say, "I'll submit to you if you submit to me." Conditional submission is not submission at all. The key to mutual submission is that both sides submit unconditionally, out of reverence for Jesus Christ.

We see submission modeled perfectly by Jesus within the Trinity. Jesus willingly submits His will to the will of God the Father. It is beautiful and it is simple—but that does *not* mean it is easy. Jesus showed us what an awful, painful, physical struggle it is to submit when he sweat blood in the Garden of Gethsemane. But he did submit by bearing his cross—along with all of our sin—and carrying it all the way up the hill called Calvary.

This means you may have to submit at times when you don't feel like it, when you don't think it's fair, when you don't think your mate is holding up his or her side of the bargain. Because it's not a "bargain" at all. It's not an "if-then" proposition—"If you could just do X, then I would gladly do Y." That's not submission. That's "let's make a deal." True submission is unconditional obedience to God's call. It's Christlike servanthood, in the covenant of marriage, clothed in mutual submission.

And if the end-goal of our mutual submission is to make sure things come out fair and even 100 percent of the time . . . we've missed the point! We've missed the point of covenant marriage—and the point of the Gospel. Christian marriage is not about what you get. It's about what you give.

Please understand, it's not easy for me to teach on this passage. When I open Ephesians 5, it's like an arctic blast of conviction hitting me right in the face. I think, "Can I get some grace here? It's not enough that I have to teach from this passage, but I have to *live* it, too!" Paul's words drive me to my knees, and all I can do is pray, "Lord, forgive my life! Forgive the times I have failed to love Bridget as You have loved the church. I'm so challenged, so guilty, and I need Your grace, I need Your Gospel!"

So if that is how you feel as you read these words of Paul, please know that you are not alone. I'm right beside you, feeling every bit as much of a failure as you do. But there's hope, there's grace, there's good news. We can't be perfect, but we can be forgiven, and we can grow toward Christlikeness and servanthood in our marriage relationships.

You may wonder, "Why is this so hard? Why is it so hard for a wife to submit to her husband? Why is it so hard for a husband to love his wife as Christ loved the church? Why is it so hard to hear the call—and why is it so hard to heed it and obey it?"

We'll answer those questions in the next chapter. But first, here's a hint: We find it hard to hear and heed the call because we do not understand the Fall.

QUESTIONS FOR STUDY OR GROUP DISCUSSION

8 | Hear the Call

1. After reading and reflecting on this chapter, would you say that your views on marriage are shaped primarily by the teaching of God's Word or by the influence of the surrounding culture? Explain your answer—and if possible, use examples.

2. The author writes, "God's call to husbands is every bit as challenging and demanding as His call to wives." Do you agree or disagree? Explain your answer, citing examples from your own experience, if possible.

3. Paul writes that our attitude should be more like Christ's. What are some of the attitudes of Christ that you need more of in your own life? How were His attitudes lived out in His actions during His earthly ministry? (To see what a Christlike attitude really looks like, read Philippians 2:1-11.)

    - What specific action steps can you take this week to demonstrate a more Christlike attitude in your relationships and your everyday life?

4. *For the wife*: Can you submit to your husband even when you don't agree? Why or why not? What specific actions or changes do you need to make to become the Christian wife God intends you to be?

5. *For the husband*: What specific actions can you take this week to become the Christian husband God intends you to be? Here are some suggestions from this chapter:

__ Become a spiritual leader. Initiate prayer and Bible study in your home.

__ Show your wife that you genuinely care about her feelings and needs.

__ Talk to her—and *listen* to her.

__ Speak positively and affirmingly *to* you wife and *about* her to others.

__ Serve your wife in active and pro-active ways.

__ Seek out her opinions. Show that you respect her thoughts and feelings.

__ Pray for her every day—and tell her you pray for her.

__ Give her thoughtful gifts and leave thoughtful notes for her.

__ Become a loving, forgiving peacemaker in your home.

__ Drop your defenses. Be willing admit that you were wrong.

__ Attend couples conferences and/or Christian marriage seminars.

__ Plan romantic getaways and weekly "date nights" with your wife.

__ Help get the kids ready for church on Sunday mornings.

9
UNDERSTAND THE FALL

God made some people male and He made some people female. Yet God made all of us, whether male or female, in His own image—so men and women are equal. As Paul writes in Galatians 3:28, "There is neither Jew nor Gentile, neither slave nor free, nor is there male and female, for you are all one in Christ Jesus."

So God made man and God made woman and they are equal—but they are *not* the same! They are equal but not equivalent, equal yet distinct. If you want proof, just watch children at play.

My son Trevor competes in junior swim meets. One time, as he and his friends awaited their turn to get into the pool, they were active and excited and they found loud, boisterous ways to burn off energy. They especially enjoyed climbing trees and waving sticks in their hands, pretending to be rulers and conquerors of all they surveyed. They were subduing the earth, as the males of the species naturally do.

But the girls on the swim team—what a difference! They sat in the shade of the tent canopy, and they talked or played quietly together. The girls didn't shout, didn't shove, didn't argue, and didn't climb trees. They made friends and related to each other as the females of the species naturally do.

So I looked up at Trevor, who was up in a tree, whooping and shouting, and I said, "Trevor, come down from there." He didn't hear me. He was too busy beating his chest and bellowing, "I'm the king!"

One of the other swim dads overheard him and laughed. Looking up at Trevor, he said, "You're the king? Who taught you that?"

"Nobody!" Trevor shouted down. "That's who I am!"

And, in a way, Trevor was right. Not about being the king. Sometimes I need to lovingly remind him that he's not the king of our household! But he was right about being a climber, an adventurer, a conqueror—a king at heart. That's how God made him.

Boys and girls are different. God made them to be different from each other. They are equal, but they are not the same.

And so it is with married couples. Husbands and wives are different. They are equal, but they are not the same. We have complementary gifts and complementary strengths and complementary roles in the midst of marriage. Neither the husband nor the wife has greater status or importance. They are equal yet distinct.

The paradoxical curse of the Fall

In order to understand why marital relationships are often so difficult, we have to understand the Fall of humanity—the moment when sin entered the human race and became an ingrained pattern of human self-will and rebellion against God. Genesis 1 and 2 tell the story of how God created the heavens and the earth and everything on the earth. God created the first man, Adam. Then God created a woman for that man.

When Adam saw the woman, Eve, he was so thrilled and enchanted with what he saw that he broke into song! We find that song recorded in Genesis 2:23. It was like a scene from a Hollywood musical. As you read the lyrics to Adam's love song, imagine those words set to a romantic show tune like "Some Enchanted Evening"—or, if you prefer, a rock love ballad like "Layla." Here is Adam's song:

> The man said,
> "This is now bone of my bones
>   and flesh of my flesh;
> she shall be called 'woman,'
>   for she was taken out of man"
> (Genesis 2:23).

Adam was captivated by Eve's beauty. Now he would no longer be alone. He had a wife to complement and complete him. Genesis goes on to tell us:

> That is why a man leaves his father and mother and is united to his wife, and they become one flesh. Adam and his wife were both naked, and they felt no shame (Genesis 2:24-25).

We human beings, in our own wayward, self-willed fashion, are always trying to get back to that "naked and unashamed" state—and we sometimes try to do so by putting our sexuality to perverted use through adultery or pornography. However, the human race can't find its own way back to the naked innocence of Eden. Why? Because of what happens next in Genesis 3.

I'm sure you know the story, but let me briefly recap the events of the Fall. The serpent—Satan in disguise—comes to Eve and asks her if God *really, truly* told her that she and Adam could not eat from any tree in the garden. (Of course, that's not what God said. He only commanded them not to eat from one particular tree.) The serpent presses Eve, planting doubts in her mind about the goodness of God, subtly urging her to rebel against God and His commands. Finally, Eve yields to the serpent's temptation—and she takes the forbidden fruit, eats it, and offers it to her husband, Adam.

The moment Adam eats the fruit, the eyes of both Adam and Eve are opened. Suddenly, they realize they are naked. And in that moment, they are ashamed of their nakedness. They sew fig leaves together to cover their nakedness—but, of course, fig leaves are a woefully inadequate covering for human nakedness.

God comes and confronts Adam and Eve because of their sin—and they try to shift the blame. In fact, Adam not only tries to blame Eve for his sin—he tries to blame God! He says, "The woman *you* put here with me—she gave me some fruit from the tree, and I ate it" (Genesis 3:12, emphasis added). In other words, "God, if *You* hadn't put this woman in my path, I never would have eaten the fruit. It's her fault—and it's *Your* fault, too!"

But Adam and Eve are left without an excuse. God tells them what the consequences of their sin shall be, beginning with the curse upon the woman:

> To the woman he said,
> "I will make your pains in childbearing very severe;
> with painful labor you will give birth to children.
> Your desire will be for your husband,
> and he will rule over you" (Genesis 3:16).

God says to the woman, "Your desire will be for your husband and he will rule over you" *because of the Fall*. That word "desire" is, in the original Hebrew, *tĕshuwqah*. It refers to a sense of longing or craving—not just in a sexual sense, but in a relational sense. To feel *tĕshuwqah*-desire is to feel incomplete without the object of that desire.

This concept of *tĕshuwqah*-desire can be visualized as a bit and reins used to guide a horse. The *tĕshuwqah*-desire of a woman is the desire for a husband to lead. Yet there is a paradox here. A woman's desire for the leadership of a man is countered by a self-willed desire to lead, a rebellion against being led (or "bossed") by someone else. There's an inner conflict at work in the heart of a woman, and this conflict is the direct result of the Fall.

As a woman, you have a desire for your husband to nurture you, protect you, provide for you, and take a leadership role—but at the same time, you want to take those reins yourself. You want your husband to be bold, firm, decisive, proactive, and manly—yet you resent it when he doesn't decide in accord with your wishes.

Tĕshuwqah means, "I love a man who takes charge! Go ahead and lead me—but I want to keep one hand on the reins myself." It means, "Honey, you drive—but drive the way I tell you! Look out! Slow down! Turn here! No, the other way! You passed it! Be careful!" That's *tĕshuwqah*.

I have a friend who felt so overwhelmed by his wife's criticism of his driving that he finally turned to her and said, "Honey, why don't you drive?

You'd obviously be so much better at it than me, so why don't we just trade places?"

Know what she said? "I think that would be best." So she drives and he sits in the passenger seat. And the explanation for *why* she drives is found right here. It's part of the curse. It's *tĕshuwqah*.

This Hebrew word *tĕshuwqah* is used to describe the desire of a woman for a man, the desire of a man for a woman—and it's also used to describe the hunger of a carnivorous animal to devour its prey. It's a desire to *consume*. It's as if you see your husband and you *want* him—but you also want to take a *bite* out of him.

Your desire will be for your husband *and* he will rule over you. He will lead you in a way that is domineering, that doesn't make sense to you, that doesn't feel right to you. And you'll *want* him to lead—yet you will also *rebel* against his leadership and you will want to lead. That is the paradoxical curse of the Fall for the woman.

A builder and cultivator

The gigantic problem that hinders all marital relationships is a problem that began with Adam and Eve. It's that continual tension a woman feels between wanting to be protected and led by a real leader—and the self-willed inner being that says, "You're not the boss of me!" This is the problem that makes it so hard for wives to submit to their husbands—and it's the problem that makes it hard for husbands to love their wives as Christ loved the church.

The problem is the Fall. The problem is original sin and its effect on our souls. Because Adam and Eve sinned, there is a curse on us all. Next, we see the curse for the man:

> To Adam he said, "Because you listened to your wife and ate fruit from the tree about which I commanded you, 'You must not eat from it,'
>
> "Cursed is the ground because of you;

> through painful toil you will eat food from it
> > all the days of your life.
> It will produce thorns and thistles for you,
> > and you will eat the plants of the field.
> By the sweat of your brow
> > you will eat your food
> until you return to the ground,
> > since from it you were taken;
> for dust you are
> > and to dust you will return" (Genesis 3:17-19).

To understand what this curse means, we have to understand the job God gave Adam even before He created Eve. God placed Adam in a beautiful garden in the middle of a wild, rugged, untamed landscape, and He said, "Look all around you, Adam. You are standing in a perfect garden. Make the whole world around you look like this garden."

In other words, God gave Adam, an unfallen man, work to do. He said, in effect, "Adam, you are going to be a builder and a cultivator. You will find meaning and self-worth in the work you do." Every godly man has that God-given purpose built into him. If you are a man, you are by nature a builder, a cultivator, a worker.

Some people think that the curse of sin is that human beings must work. But the Genesis story makes it clear that, even before sin entered the world, God gave human beings work to do—and it was pleasant, fulfilling, meaningful work. All honest work is honoring to God, and work itself is not a "curse" caused by sin. Work is God's gift to an unfallen humanity.

But after sin entered the world, everything became marred by sin. Even God's gift of work became bitter and cursed. God told Adam, "The very things you are called to build and cultivate and work on will at times war against you. You will plant seed and cultivate the ground, but the ground itself will war against you with weeds and pests and drought, and you will be engaged in a continual war with the earth just to grow your food. You will try to cultivate a relationship with your wife and children, but you'll continually have to deal with marital conflict and misbehaving, rebellious children. They will war against you."

This is the curse. This is the Fall. This is who we are. That's why it's so hard for wives to submit to their husbands, and for husbands to love their wives as Christ loved the church.

Eternal truth in a nutshell

But the story of the Fall does not end there.

God enabled us to be healed of this curse. He placed the curse and the penalty for our sin on Jesus. We see the first glimmering of the Gospel right here in the opening chapters of Genesis, in the very first pages of the Bible. God addresses the serpent that tempted Adam and Eve and pronounces a curse—and a prediction:

> So the LORD God said to the serpent,
> "Because you have done this,
>   "Cursed are you above all livestock
>   and all wild animals!
> You will crawl on your belly
>   and you will eat dust
>   all the days of your life.
> And I will put enmity
>   between you and the woman,
>   and between your offspring and hers;
> he will crush your head,
>   and you will strike his heel" (Genesis 3:14-15).

At first glance, you might think that God is telling the serpent, "Because of what you did, people are going to hate snakes and try to kill them, and snakes are going to bite people." But with the hindsight of biblical history, we can see another, more profound interpretation: The offspring of the woman is Jesus, the son of Mary, descended from Eve. On the cross, the serpent (a symbol of Satan) strikes His heel, piercing him with the nails of the crucifixion—but at the same time, Jesus, through His death and resurrection, crushes the head of Satan, destroying the power of sin and death.

God's curse upon Satan in Genesis 3:15 is the Gospel compressed to a few lines of poetic imagery. It's eternal truth in a nutshell.

Here, in the opening verses of the first book of the Bible, we see both our need of a Savior—and God's promise of a Savior. The original sin of Adam and Eve creates a problem that only the birth, life, death, and resurrection of Jesus Christ can solve. We all wrestle with the curse of sin. We wrestle with it in our marriages, in our family relationships, and in the inner struggles of our own souls.

When we understand the Fall, we understand the curse—and we better understand some of the underlying struggles and tensions in the marriage relationship. The curse of the Fall is an explanation for why it is so hard for us to submit to one another in marriage. It's an explanation—but not an excuse.

Now that we have heard the call, now that we better understand the Fall, it's time for us to learn how to "hold the ball."

QUESTIONS FOR STUDY OR GROUP DISCUSSION

9 | Understand the Fall

1. *For the wife*: God said to Eve, "Your desire will be for your husband and he will rule over you" because of the Fall. Do you identify with the effects of the Fall, as described in Genesis 3? Do you feel an inner tension between wanting to be led by a "real man" and wanting to rebel against a man's leadership? Why or why not? Explain your answer with examples.

2. *For the husband:* Do you identify with the effects of the Fall, as described in Genesis 3? Do you feel you were created to work and build and accomplish things, but at the same time you feel that work is a struggle and sometimes even a curse? Do you feel that your career wars against you? Explain your answer with examples.

3. In Genesis 3:12, when God confronted Adam and Eve about their sin, Adam replied, "The woman *you* put here with me—she gave me some fruit from the tree, and I ate it." In other words, Adam seems to blame God for his own problems. Have you ever blamed God for the problems you are going through?

   - What does this passage say to you about blaming God versus taking personal responsibility for your own sins?

4. What insights into man-woman relationships do you find in the story of the Fall? Does this story help you to see why it is so hard for wives to submit to their husbands, and for husbands to love their wives as Christ loved the church? Why or why not?

5. The Bible teaches that men and women are equal, but not equivalent. Do you agree or disagree with this view of gender roles?

6. Are your attitudes toward gender roles shaped largely by the Bible or by the influence of your culture?

10
HOLD THE BALL

When I played football at UCLA, each practice was divided into twelve periods of five to fifteen minutes each. For the first half of every practice, we divided up into position groups (I played wide receiver), and all backs and receivers devoted one entire period each day to a drill called Ball Security. A football has an unusual shape and size that creates special problems for the person carrying the ball. So the Ball Security drill was designed to make players aware the proper technique for holding the ball to prevent a costly fumble. You have to hold the ball with multiple points of pressure, because your opponent is constantly trying to strip the ball from your hands or force you to fumble.

In the same way, husbands and wives need to learn how to "hold the ball" to keep from fumbling away their marriage relationship. In this chapter, we're going to see what God's Word teaches about how to "hold the ball" in covenant marriage. We'll learn how to "hold the ball" with grace and how to embrace the Gospel as it relates to our marriage relationships. We'll learn the different "pressure points" in marriage, and how to use those pressure points to make our marriages firm and secure.

How do we do that? How do we make a marriage stable, secure, and honoring to God?

First pressure point: Mastering the art of submission

If you're going to secure the "ball" of marriage, you must know how to manage the first pressure point—mastering the art of submission. We return to that challenging passage, Ephesians 5:22: "Wives, submit yourselves to your own husbands as you do to the Lord." Why does Paul start by giving this word of counsel to wives?

I believe Paul addresses wives first in Ephesians 5:22 because no man can lead a woman who is not willing to follow. And lets face it: All of us, both men and women, resist the idea of submission. If you inwardly rebel against what Paul says in Ephesians 5, I don't blame you. I empathize with you. I know how hard it is to submit to someone else in any arena of life.

As a wife, you may say, "You don't know my husband. You don't know how he treats me." And at this point, I think I should make one point clear: If you are experiencing abuse or violence in your marriage, please go to the Appendix at the end of this book and read the "Note to Victims of Abuse." This book deals with problems that fall into the normal range of marital stresses and conflicts. But if there is abuse or violence in your marriage, that's definitely not normal. You need immediate help. Nowhere does God's Word suggest that you should submit to abuse or violence.

Having said that, I know it's hard for a wife to obey God's call to submit even to a loving and thoughtful Christian husband. But when you, as a wife, are called to submit to your husband, please understand that your submission is not based on his merit. It's based on God's mercy. Wives are called to submit to their husbands "as to the Lord." Submission to your husband is a way of worshipping the Lord and showing reverence to Him.

So, in essence, a wife does not have to focus on her husband and his merit (or lack of merit). Her focus is on God the Father and His Son, Jesus Christ, and on all that the Lord has done for her. She says, "I will obey the Lord in the midst of my marriage relationship. And whether my husband is worthy of it or not, whether he is a Christian or not, I will submit to him, willingly and lovingly." If you can submit to God in your relationship with Him, then you know what it takes to submit to your husband.

A Christlike attitude of submission is a powerful witness for Christ. As the apostle Paul writes, "How do you know, wife, whether you will save your husband? Or, how do you know, husband, whether you will save your wife?" (1 Corinthians 7:16). But if you cannot submit to God, then I promise you that you'll have a real struggle trying to submit to your husband.

Proverbs 12:4 presents to us with two contrasting images of a wife. The first half of that verse tells us, "A wife of noble character is her husband's crown." A godly wife is so pleasing and noble that she is like a crown upon her husband's brow—the crown jewel of his life. Everyone sees how capable, winsome, and beautiful she is in every way. That is one kind of wife.

The second kind of wife is described for us in such verses as Proverbs 25:24—"Better to live on a corner of the roof than share a house with a quarrelsome wife." Or Proverbs 27:15—"A quarrelsome wife is like the dripping of a leaky roof in a rainstorm." Or the second half of Proverbs 12:4—"but a disgraceful wife is like decay in his bones." These are vivid word pictures describing the intense suffering an ungodly, ungracious wife inflicts on her husband. She's like the constant ache of decaying bones or the relentless drip, drip, dripping of a leaky roof. In fact, a man is better off living on one little corner of a rooftop than to live beneath that roof with a wife who makes him miserable.

So, if you are a wife, the question for you is: "Am I going to be the crown on my husband's brow—or the decay in his bones? Am I going to be an abiding source of honor and pride for my husband—or a source of pain?" This constant question is a key pressure point in marriage. When you obey God's command—and take steps toward mastering the art of submission—you are "holding the ball" obediently in your marriage. And you will be blessed.

As the wife, you may be thinking, "All right, get off my case! When are you going to tell my husband how a godly husband is supposed to live and lead?" That's a fair question, because the apostle Paul spends the majority of his time speaking to husbands—and so will I.

Second pressure point: Wives *LOVE* love

The second pressure point in securing the "ball" of marriage is understanding how women think about love. And husband, I'm talking now to you, man to man.

As men, we need to acknowledge that it's hard for a woman—even the godliest of women—to submit to her husband. And as men, we have to own some of the responsibility for making this challenge even harder for our wives. One of the main reasons it's so hard for the women in our lives to submit is that *we are terrible leaders.*

We don't lead like Christ, we don't love like Christ, we don't forgive like Christ, we don't serve like Christ, we are not others-centered like Christ. Any leader who does not lead like Christ is a bad leader. So our wives look at us and say, "Are you saying God wants me to submit myself to *that*? Come on!"

So you and I need to own that right now. We are part of the submission problem our wives face. God, speaking through Paul, says, "Husbands, love your wives, just as Christ loved the church and gave himself up for her to make her holy." How do we do this? What are some practical ways we can become the kind of husbands God meant us to be? How can we acquire the tools to truly love, *love*, *LOVE* our wives?

(Excuse me, ma'am, but I know you're reading what I'm writing to your husband—so let me ask you: Wouldn't you just *love* it if your husband loved you as Christ loved the church? Yes, I thought so.)

Husband, let me tell you something about wives. I've been married to Bridget for a decade, and this is what I know about my wife (and let me tell you, this is true of *all* wives, including *your* wife):

Wives *LOVE* love!

Isn't that true? They *can't get enough* of love! I can't remember the last movie I got to pick for Bridget and me to watch. It's been years. Bridget picks the movie, and it's always a love story. They don't call 'em "chick flicks" for nothing. They're lovey and dovey and gooey and drippy with love, because wives *LOVE* love!

If you walk into a card section in a store, how many guys do you see there? None! It's all women. And the women are getting choked up over cards about love. A woman will spend $10 on a card if it has a really beautiful sentiment about love. But guys? We go to the 99-cent section and we look for a card that makes us laugh. It's seems a little steep, but okay, we'll spend a buck for a funny card. It's a guy thing—and that's one of the differences between husbands and wives.

Bridget and I have been trying to eliminate TV from our family life to allow time for more worthwhile activities. But around the middle of summer, a horrible thought struck me. "Whoa, whoa, whoa!" I said. "I just realized that football season starts in late August, and we shouldn't be too hasty about eliminating TV during football season!"

So I got a little carve-out, a little exception, for football season. One night, after the kids were in bed, I was catching the football highlights on SportsCenter, and Bridget was checking Facebook on the laptop. "Oh, this is so cute!" she said. "Tyler, you've got to see this!"

So I reluctantly pulled myself away from SportsCenter and I looked at the Facebook page. The name on the page was unfamiliar to me. I asked, "Do you know this person?"

"No. It's the friend of a friend of a friend. But look at this video. This man is proposing to his wife."

"A man we don't know, proposing to a woman we don't know?" I thought, *Are you serious?* I really didn't want to watch it—but I knew I would be speaking at church about marriage and mutual submission, so I said, "Honey, let's watch it together."

Bridget brought the laptop over and set it in front of us and clicked "play." And we watched a three-minute video of a guy proposing to a young lady, and it said "I Love You" across the screen in flowing script and there was a border of hearts and flowers around the screen. I thought, *Okay, I guess it's a little cute but it's really kind of cheesy.*

(If you're the guy who made the video, then I take it back. You're a romantic guy, an example to all husbands, I admire you, and I need to become more like you.)

When it was over, I looked at Bridget—and remember, she had already watched it a couple of times—and she was sniffling and her eyes were wet with tears. I was really surprised because, for a girl, she doesn't really get that emotional. I thought, *Are you kidding me?*

Husband, *that* is what we are dealing with! Our wives *LOVE* love—and the challenge for you and me as husbands is to become the kind of godly husbands who love our wives the way our wives love to be loved.

Third pressure point: Husband, be the initiator

The third pressure point in holding the "ball" is that you, husband, must be the initiator. How do our wives want to be loved? They truly want to be loved as Christ loved the church. So in loving our wives, we need to follow Christ's lead.

How did Jesus love the church? He initiated! He gave Himself up for the us even while we were in rebellion against Him, even while we rejected Him. So you and I must initiate acts of love, forgiveness, and reconciliation toward our wives—even in those times when communication is broken, when there is hurt and anger on both sides. Jesus initiated—and so must we.

Jesus also rescued the church. He served the church and became sin for the church. He willingly allowed his own body to be pierced, flayed, and torn apart for the church. He does everything for the church—not because the church has asked for help, not because the church deserves to be rescued, but because it is His nature to initiate love and rescue.

Husband, initiate! Initiate, initiate, initiate! You be the one who initiates healing and grace. You be the one who swallows pride and initiates the apology. You be the one who says, "I was wrong. Please forgive me. I love you and I don't want any barriers to exist between us."

Not, "I was wrong, but—" Not, "We were wrong—" Not, "Mistakes were made," but "I was wrong," period.

Now, I know how these husband-and-wife disputes go. You argue, and the argument ends without resolution. And what does she do? She goes to bed. Her head hits the pillow and she's out. And you're awake, you're fuming, your blood is boiling, you're thinking of all kinds of brilliant comebacks you *wish* you'd said—and *she went to bed*! You're stuck with a big lump of resentment in your belly and what do you do?

Then you remember the counsel of Ephesians 4:26—"Do not let the sun go down while you are still angry." So you go into the bedroom and you give her a little nudge and say, "Honey, I want you to know that I was wrong. Please forgive me." Not, "I apologize, but—" Not, "I apologize if—" A qualified apology just won't do. An apology must be abject and unconditional or it's not an apology.

In that moment, you may think that it's 99.9999 percent her fault and 0.0001 percent your fault. It doesn't matter. No ifs, ands, or buts—apologize, period. If the two of you are able to calmly, rationally discuss the matter (preferably in the morning, when you are both less tired and more reasonable), and you are able to hear her side of the argument more objectively, you just might find that the fault is shared a lot more equally than you realized in the heat of the moment.

As a man, as a husband who seeks to love his wife as Christ loved the church, you initiate the apology. You initiate reconciliation and repentance. If there is work to be done in the relationship, you initiate it. If there is prayer to be offered, you initiate it. What did Christ do for His bride? He initiated.

If you want to love like Christ, then initiate in the relationship with your wife.

Fourth pressure point: Husband, nourish and nurture

The fourth pressure point in securing the "ball" is that you, husband, must nourish and nurture your wife. In Ephesians 5, the apostle Paul appeals to our self-interest, explaining that when we, as husbands, love our wives, we are really showing the highest love to ourselves. He writes:

> In this same way, husbands ought to love their wives as their own bodies. He who loves his wife loves himself. After all, no one ever hated their own body, but they feed and care for their body, just as Christ does the church—for we are members of his body (Ephesians 5:28-30).

We feed and care for our own bodies. We nourish ourselves. In the same way, we men ought to nourish our wives as we nourish ourselves. He who loves his wife loves himself. The original New Testament word for "feed" or "nourish" in this passage is used to describe how a loving father cares for his children and provides for them. There is a sense of provision and protection in this word that is both physical and spiritual in nature.

First, there is the issue of physical nurture and nourishment. What I'm about to say will be controversial. I believe God's Word teaches that husbands have the primary responsibility to work outside the home and provide for their families. That doesn't mean that wives can't be the primary breadwinners for a limited time and for a specific purpose, particularly if there are no children involved.

During the first two years of our marriage, I studied at Fuller Theological Seminary in order to complete my Masters of Divinity degree. Bridget was the primary breadwinner, working full-time as a chiropractor. I was a full-time student, part-time waiter, and (it's true) a part-part-time contestant on *The Price Is Right*.

In the spring of 2002, about a year into our marriage, Bridget and I were living in Southern California. She was working and I was in grad school. Bridget's parents came out from the Midwest for a few days. Bridget had to work, but I was able to take my in-laws to a taping of *The Price is Right*.

Early in the show, the announcer called, "Tyler Scott, come on down!" I was a contestant! Right off the bat, I bid on some his-and-hers Bugs Bunny bowling equipment—and won the bid! That got me up onstage.

Host Bob Barker asked me about myself, and I told him I was a pastor and that my wife's parents were in the audience. Then we played the Grand Money Game. I started out with a dollar. To win the big money, I had to correctly pick four grocery store items that sold for under five dollars. If I picked one of the items priced over five dollars, I'd lose.

One by one, I picked the first three items correctly—and Bob Barker stopped me and gave me a chance to walk away from the game with $1,000 guaranteed—or I could risk everything I'd already won and press on for the $10,000 prize. "Bob," I said, "I didn't wait in line for all those hours before the show just to walk away now. I'm going for the ten grand!"

I consulted with the audience on the fourth grocery item, I milked the moment—and I made the correct call. I won the $10,000!

The crowd went crazy—and so did I!

Moments later, I spun the big wheel for the Showcase Showdown—and it landed on one dollar—which meant an additional $1000 in cash, plus a bonus spin. My next spin landed on the nickel, which was good for another $5000!

All told, I won $16,000 in cash (plus the bowling balls) in the space of just ten minutes. (For some reason, I never got around to picking up the bowling balls—a mistake I regret.) That ten minutes of game show exposure paid for a whole year of grad school!

And I was pleased that it all happened right in front of my mother- and father-in-law, who looked on with shock and awe! After the show, we drove straight from the CBS studio in Hollywood to Bridget's chiropractic office in Huntington Beach. I called her out to the parking lot, and with her folks at my side, I told her, "Babe, we had a *big* day—a very, very *BIG* day!"

Now, is there a point to that story? Actually, there is.

The first few years of our marriage were a work-and-study season in our lives. Bridget worked full-time, and I studied full-time and waited tables part-time (plus, in a way neither of us could have planned or anticipated, the Lord blessed my appearance on a TV game show). Bridget and I carefully, prayerfully planned that arrangement, and we promised each other that it would only be for a limited time, and for a specific purpose—to get me through grad school. Today Bridget is a full-time mom to three young boys, and she is also a part-time chiropractor. Quite frankly, I don't know how she does it.

I'm not trying to inflict guilt on you if your family honestly can't make it without two full-time salaries. But I know that many couples who *think* they need two fulltime paychecks could actually get by with less by foregoing that new car, boat, expensive vacation, restaurant dining, or status symbol house. We think we need more income, when we merely want more stuff. Spending less money on stuff could enable Mom to spend more time with the kids during the crucial developmental stages of their lives.

Working moms often fail to figure all the costs of being employed. When travel expenses, daycare, wardrobe, and other costs are factored in, many women are surprised to discover that it doesn't make financial sense for them to work outside the home.

Part of being a godly husband and loving my wife as Christ loved the church means providing food, clothing, and shelter. That's what it means to nourish and nurture. Men build and cultivate primarily at work. Women build and cultivate primarily in the home. No couple should ever feel guilty for doing what they need to in difficult times, but as Christians we should make sure we are not rationalizing away our responsibilities to our families and to God.

I can hear some women saying, "We live in an era when women are free to do anything that men do. Now you come along and say to women, 'Get back into the kitchen where you belong.' What gives you the right to relegate women to second-fiddle status?"

And my reply to that question is another question: "Since when is being a homemaker and a full-time mother 'second-fiddle'? When did being a mother become something less honorable than being, say, a CEO, an account executive, or a teacher? What has happened to our society that the role of a full-time mother lost the respect and prestige it once deservedly enjoyed?"

I look at full-time moms and I think they are doing the hardest, the most humbling, most difficult, most rewarding and fulfilling job on this planet. I've tried being "mom" to my kids just one day a week. On Fridays, when Bridget works until 3 p.m., the kids are mine from morning until Bridget comes home. Our three boys are wonderful, but they are full of energy and they can think up a thousand ways to make life challenging.

One day a week, I get a taste of what Bridget deals with the rest of the week. So the rest of the week, when I get home from work, and Bridget meets me at the door with that wild look in her eyes that says, *I'm right on the edge from dealing with YOUR boys all day long*, I know exactly how she feels. I can relate to her crazed look or her clenched teeth. She needs a little time alone.

I call out, "Okay, boys! Let's go, let's go, let's go." We pile in the van, and in seconds we're on the road to the park or the local high school football field to burn off some energy—and Bridget's on the road to recovery.

It's my job as the husband to nourish and nurture my wife, to give her some time to physically recover from the challenges of being a mostly stay-at-home mom.

And as the husband, it's also my job to nourish my wife and children spiritually. This means I have a responsibility to call the family together for prayer and Bible reading. I have a responsibility to initiate a conversation with my wife and children about what God is doing in their lives, and to talk about how I relate to God on a daily basis in my own life.

As men, you and I can't offer nourishment to our families if our own spiritual cup is empty. We have to be continually filling our cup from God's Word if we're going to have anything to offer our families. We have to be continually filling our cup with God's wisdom, insight, faith, love, and hope, so that we have the spiritual nourishment to offer others.

Fifth pressure point: Husband, cherish your wife

The fifth pressure point in holding the "ball" is that you, husband, must cherish your wife. Paul writes that a loving husband feeds and cares for—that is, he cherishes—his wife as he cares for his own body.

We find this same term used in 1 Peter 3:7, where the apostle Peter says, "Husbands, in the same way be considerate as you live with your wives, and treat them with respect as the weaker partner and as heirs with you of the gracious gift of life, so that nothing will hinder your prayers." In other words, Peter says a godly husband is to be considerate and gentle, cherishing his wife because she is the "weaker partner."

Now, Peter isn't saying that women are weak and frail. He's saying that women are delicate, like priceless porcelain—beautiful yet breakable. Porcelain is a ceramic material made of clay with glass and other minerals that make it hard, strong, and translucent, but also brittle and fragile when it is handled roughly. Women, like porcelain, have many strengths—but should not be treated roughly. As husbands, we need to be gentle with our words and our actions. We need to cherish our wives.

Do you cherish your wife? To cherish is to cultivate an environment of intimacy. I know that the idea of intimacy scares many guys—but intimacy is the goal of cherishing. To love your wife intimately, you must know her specifically. This means you have to take time to listen to her, observe her, study her, pray with her, and learn her love languages (see Chapter 5).

Do you know your wife's love language? Does she like physical touch? Sometimes Bridget likes touch. Specifically, she likes a foot rub. We'll be sitting on the couch together, and she's had a hard day at work or at home with the kids—or both. And I'll be watching TV or reading a book, and suddenly—

There's her foot, right in my lap. I look at her and say, "Really?"

And she says, "Really."

So it's time to rub her foot. That's what she likes, and I want to love her the way she wants to be loved.

Does your wife like time—quality time with you? Do you and your wife have a regular date night? Ours is on Fridays. My mom comes over to baby-sit the boys (they call her "Gamma"). Or we take them to her house. If my mom's not available, we sometimes hire a sitter. You may not have a built-in baby-sitter like we do, and you may say, "Hiring a sitter is steep! I can't afford it!"

I'd say you can't afford *not* to date your wife and give her the gift of your time. It really is that important. You may need to say no to a round of golf or an evening of racquetball. You may need to brown-bag your lunches or cut back on the Starbucks to make room in the budget. Whatever it takes, invest time in your relationship with your wife. Date her consistently, regularly, creatively, passionately.

Fellas, I recommend a three-pronged approach to dating your wife. Life is very busy, so you have to fight to do the following three things:

- ***Get Consistent.*** Establish a regular pattern of dates. One of the hardest things to do on a regular basis once you start a family is to keep dating your wife. But consistency in dating is music to a marriage.
- ***Get Creative.*** Use your imagination and all your resources (the Internet, your friends, restaurant reviews, and so forth) to creatively date your mate. "Creative" doesn't have to mean "expensive." A little cash and a lot of thoughtfulness can go a long way.
- ***Get Carried Away.*** A couple times each year (anniversaries and her birthday are easy wins), take her to meaningful place. Stay a night in a hotel. Whisk her away for a day. Again, this can be done with aplomb, even on a pint-sized budget.

(Ladies, do I hear an "Amen"?)

The process of dating does not begin with getting in the car to leave for a date. It begins with establishing healthy patterns of making time for your wife and family.

How do you make time? Well, you could spend less time on the Internet, reading the paper, watching ESPN, or talking on the phone. When I'm spending time with my family, I try not to just put my phone on vibrate. I try to shut it off completely. I almost never answer my phone at the dinner table or when I'm in the backyard with my boys. When I'm with my wife and kids, I'm *with* my wife and kids, period.

I have some friends who call me, and there are times when I just love to hit the "reject" button when they call. It doesn't just go to voice mail, they get a message that they've been rejected! And they know why, because it's my way of telling them, "Yeah, I'm choosing my wife over you guys!" I'm close with these guys, so I can do that. Sometimes, you just have to say no to your friends, no to your work, no to the TV, or no to the golf course, because you want to invest time in your most important relationship. Your wife needs your time, and you choose to give her what she needs.

Maybe your wife needs an act of service. If so, then serve her the way she likes to be served. I have a phrase that may help you: *Power through the honey-do*. If she gives you a honey-do list, just make up your mind to put your head down and power through that bad boy.

Or maybe your wife needs gifts. My father-in-law, Bridget's dad, is the most caring and thoughtful man I know. He gives gifts to his wife all the time. He continually pays attention to her needs, then he meets those needs. They live in Minnesota, where it is bitterly cold in the wintertime. When he finds out that she is getting ready to go out in the car, he doesn't wait to be asked. He goes out, starts the car, and gets the heater warmed up for her. In the summertime, he goes out and gets the air conditioner running for her. My mother-in-law never steps into a car that is too cold or too hot, because her husband knows exactly the gift she needs.

The gift you give doesn't need to expensive. It doesn't have to cost anything at all. It only needs to be an expression of your thoughtfulness and your love.

Does your wife need talk? Does she need the gift of *rhema*, the gift of face-time with you, just talking and being listened to? I recall one Saturday morning after our Friday date night. We had one hour before Mom brought the kids back, and Bridget said, "Let's go for a walk downtown and get a cup of coffee. Let's just talk."

Well, that was not what I had planned. I wanted to sit at home and read the paper. But I said (and I'm sure Bridget heard the lack of enthusiasm in my voice), "That would be lovely."

So off we went. And we were talking, just talking, and we got coffee. As we were walking home, taking our time, I asked Bridget questions—and she was just blooming! She was spunky and smiling and as happy as I've ever seen her. And I remember thinking, *This is too easy! Is this really all she needs to make her happy?*

Yet talk is what Bridget wanted. Wives just want to be awash in *rhema*, in speech—because when you listen to her, she knows you care. She knows you love her. So give her the love she wants. If you don't know what kind of love she wants, ask her.

That is how we "hold the ball." These are the "pressure points" that enable us to secure the marriage relationship so that we don't fumble away this gift God has given us. Wives, you help secure the marriage through godly acts of submission. Husbands, you help secure the marriage through your love for your wife, through initiating in marriage, through nourishing and cherishing your wife and family.

Finally, a word to wives: If you, as a wife, have a husband who is not the kind of man I've described above, please be patient. Wait for him. Pray for him. Submit to him and respect him, even when he's not worthy of respect.

Do that out of reverence for Christ. Do that, God says, and he will become respectable.

And a final word to husbands: If you, as a husband, have a difficult wife who does not submit to you now, please be patient. Wait for her. Pray for her. Love your wife even when she's not worthy of love. Love her out of reverence for Christ. And love her as Christ loved the church. Initiate love. Do this, God says, and she will become lovable.

Husbands and wives, we have that power to build up, to bless, to pray, to love. That's the ball, and our challenge is to hold the ball, to secure the ball against all the forces that would try to strip it away and make us fumble.

So run to daylight with that ball. Honor God with your marriage.

QUESTIONS FOR STUDY OR GROUP DISCUSSION

10 | Hold the Ball

1. Why is it hard for women to master the art of submission? Is it the wife's fault—or the husband's? Or neither? Or both? Explain your answer.

2. Is there enough romance—the kind of love that wives love—in your marriage? Why or why not?

   - What needs to happen or change in order for both of you to be happy with the depth of romantic experience in your marriage?

3. Who is the initiator in your marriage? What (if anything) do you need to do differently in order for the husband to be the initiator in your relationship?

4. Who is the nourisher and nurturer in your marriage? What (if anything) do you need to do differently in order for the husband to assume the nourisher and nurturer role in your relationship?

5. Does the wife in your marriage experience being cherished by the husband? Why or why not? What (if anything) can you do to improve that situation?

11
WIN THE CROWD!

When Bridget and I were married, I stood at the front of the church and Bridget's father walked with her down the aisle. Before all of those assembled witnesses, her father symbolically gave her hand to me. What does this significant symbol in the wedding ceremony mean? It's a picture of God the Father presenting the church to His Son.

The wedding ceremony and marriage itself are filled with images that reflect the truth of the Christian Gospel. When we as Christians honor and live out God's plan for Christian marriage, we bear witness in front of a watching world, in front of the crowd around us, what the good news of the Gospel really is, and what it truly means to be members of the church, the bride of Christ.

Just as God has committed Himself to a relationship with His people through a covenant, a husband and wife commit to each other through a covenant. In marriage, the bride takes the name of her husband and becomes identified with him, just as we Christians take on the name of Christ and become identified with Him. The bride's submission to her husband mirrors the church's obedience to the lordship of Jesus Christ. The husband's initiating, self-sacrificing, protective leadership role in the marriage mirrors Christ's relationship with the church. Christian husbands are to love their wives even more than their own bodies, just as Christ loved the church and gave Himself for her.

Covenant marriage requires faithfulness. It's an exclusive relationship. The two marriage partners pledge themselves to each other exclusively and for all time. They do not look up old flames on Facebook. They do not entertain lustful thoughts about other people in the office or the neighborhood. The very notion of unfaithfulness is an unthinkable violation of the marriage covenant. These principles of covenant marriage reflect the fact that God exclusively and jealously loves us and wants us for His own (see Exodus 43:14), and anyone who flirts with false religions, occultism, and other God-substitutes is guilty of spiritual adultery.

The marriage relationship naturally produces children and makes the human race fruitful. God desires that the church of Jesus Christ also be fruitful, producing spiritual "offspring" by attracting new followers, by making new disciples. Christians are expected by God to spiritually procreate just as married couples physically procreate.

In covenant marriage, a man and a woman come together in a safe and protective enclosure where they can be naked and unashamed. They know each other completely, including their faults, flaws, and secrets, yet they feel safe, knowing they are loved unconditionally. Every human soul longs for this kind of intimacy—the same level of intimacy that exists between Christ and His bride, the church. The Lord knows all of our sins and secrets—yet He loves us unconditionally and gave His life for us.

As C. J. Mahaney writes in *Sex, Romance, and the Glory of God*, "All Christian marriages are intended ultimately to point to that greater reality. The final, glorious purpose of Christian marriage is to witness to the relationship between Christ and the Church."[1] Covenant marriage is one of the means God uses to tell the Gospel story to the world. Through covenant marriage, we live out the Gospel before the crowd around us, and one of our goals in marriage is to win the crowd—*our* crowd—for Christ.

What is the Gospel?

Marriage, says the apostle Paul, is a profound mystery. A lot of married people would agree that marriage can be a perplexing and mystifying state of being—but that's not what Paul means. He writes:

> "For this reason a man will leave his father and mother and be united to his wife, and the two will become one flesh." This is a profound mystery—but I am talking about Christ and the church. However, each one of you also must love his wife as he loves himself, and the wife must respect her husband (Ephesians 5:31-33).

Notice that after he describes marriage, he says, "This is a profound mystery"—then he quickly adds, "but I am talking about Christ and the church." The part of marriage that is so mysterious and profound is that *marriage is a picture of Christ and His church*. In other words, marriage is a picture of the Gospel, the good news of Jesus Christ for a broken and dying world.

Now, Paul is not saying that marriage is *nothing but* a picture of the Gospel, nor is he saying that *only* marriage is a picture of the Gospel. He's saying that God has chosen to depict the spiritual reality of the Gospel through the image and symbolism of marriage. When two godly people, a man and a woman, come together and create a godly covenant marriage relationship, God is able to work through that relationship to win the people around them to Himself.

Let me express this idea succinctly: *We must live the Gospel out loud in order to win the crowd.* That's the theme of the three concluding chapters of this book. This theme can be broken down into three key questions:

1. What is the Gospel?
2. Who is our crowd?
3. How do we live the Gospel out loud?

I believe that after we have explored these three questions together, you will never look at your marriage relationship in quite the same way again. As we look at these questions, join me in inviting the Holy Spirit to open our hearts and help us to experience what it really means to have our marriages transformed into living witnesses to God's love and grace.

The question we focus on in this chapter is Question 1: What is the Gospel? This question is not as simple as it seems.

The Gospel is the good news that saves us, that binds us together as followers of Christ, as believers, as His church. The Gospel is the very heart of the Christian faith. But what is the good news of the Gospel? I believe that many people who call themselves Christians don't really know what the Gospel is.

All the religions in the world except Christianity have one operating principle, and it is this: *Obey the god you serve so that you will be accepted.* If you follow the precepts of your religion, if you keep its laws and obey its rites and rituals, then your hope is that, at the end of your life, the deity of that religion will accept you. Many people think this is how Christianity works, but that's simply not true.

The Christian Gospel, the good news of Jesus Christ, is that you are accepted by God's grace. You don't have to keep a set of rules or rituals in order to be accepted. In fact, you are incapable of keeping God's laws—and He understands that. The Psalmist wrote, "For he knows how we are formed, he remembers that we are dust (Psalm 103:14). And Paul tells us, "For all have sinned and fall short of the glory of God (Romans 3:23).

The goal of every other religion is to earn your way to God. But Christianity says you *cannot* earn your way to God. You are not accepted by God based on your own good works, but based on the work Jesus did for you on the cross. As Paul explains, "For it is by grace you have been saved, through faith—and this is not from yourselves, it is the gift of God—not by works, so that no one can boast" (Ephesians 2:8-9).

You can't earn salvation. You can only accept it by grace through faith as a free gift. Once you understand the Gospel, your entire motivation for following God is transformed. Instead of doing good works to win God's acceptance (and never being sure if you have done enough), you obey God out of a heart full of gratitude for the salvation He has given to you *as a free gift* of His love and grace.

What is the Gospel? The Gospel is everything. It's the motivation for everything you do. It's your reason for living. It's the reason you love your spouse and children. It's the message you share with friends, family, and neighbors. It's the motive for the time you spend volunteering, for the money you donate, for the people you help along the way. It's the reason you gather with fellow Christians to pray and worship God. The Gospel is all-encompassing, all-empowering, all-motivating.

The Gospel is everything.

We are wayward and unrighteous

There is an amazing consistency between the Old Testament and the New Testament. In the Old Testament book of Ezekiel, for example, we find a profound foreshadowing of the Christian Gospel. Ezekiel 16 depicts a wedding story that illustrates the relationship between Christ and His church. I believe the apostle Paul, being steeped in the Old Testament as a Jew among Jews, had this passage from Ezekiel in mind when the Holy Spirit inspired him to write Ephesians 5:

> On the day you were born your cord was not cut, nor were you washed with water to make you clean, nor were you rubbed with salt or wrapped in cloths. No one looked on you with pity or had compassion enough to do any of these things for you. Rather, you were thrown out into the open field, for on the day you were born you were despised.
>
> Then I passed by and saw you kicking about in your blood, and as you lay there in your blood I said to you, "Live!" I made you grow like a plant of the field. You grew and developed and entered puberty. Your breasts had formed and your hair had grown, yet you were stark naked.

> Later I passed by, and when I looked at you and saw that you were old enough for love, I spread the corner of my garment over you and covered your naked body. I gave you my solemn oath and entered into a covenant with you, declares the Sovereign Lord, and you became mine (Ezekiel 16:4-8).

Here again, we see a picture of covenant marriage. God finds us in a helpless and abused state. We are incapable of doing anything to save ourselves. Yet He gives us life, He gives us grace, He makes a covenant with us that He alone can keep. "I gave you my solemn oath and entered into a covenant with you," God tells us, "and you became mine." We became His—just as a husband belongs to his wife and a wife belongs to her husband. Ezekiel continues:

> "'I bathed you with water and washed the blood from you and put ointments on you. I clothed you with an embroidered dress and put sandals of fine leather on you. I dressed you in fine linen and covered you with costly garments. I adorned you with jewelry: I put bracelets on your arms and a necklace around your neck, and I put a ring on your nose, earrings on your ears and a beautiful crown on your head. So you were adorned with gold and silver; your clothes were of fine linen and costly fabric and embroidered cloth. Your food was honey, olive oil and the finest flour. You became very beautiful and rose to be a queen. And your fame spread among the nations on account of your beauty, because the splendor I had given you made your beauty perfect, declares the Sovereign Lord (Ezekiel 16:9-14).

That is the good news! That is the Gospel to you and me: God chooses you, God loves you, God washes you, God pursues you, God makes His covenant with you.

And how did we respond to the Gospel, to the love and grace God has showered upon us? Ezekiel writes:

> "'But you trusted in your beauty and used your fame to become a prostitute. You lavished your favors on anyone who passed by and your beauty became his. You took some of your garments to make gaudy high places, where you carried on your prostitution. You went to him, and he possessed your beauty. You also took the fine jewelry I gave you, the jewelry made of my gold and silver, and you made for yourself male idols and engaged in prostitution with them. And you took your embroidered clothes to put on them, and you offered my oil and incense before them. Also the food I provided for you—the flour, olive oil and honey I gave you to eat—you offered as fragrant incense before them. That is what happened, declares the Sovereign LORD (Ezekiel 16:15-19).

In other words, the Lord says to us, "You took the blessings I poured out on you and the gifts I gave you and all your bling—and you thought it was all for you!" The Lord's indictment continues:

> "'And you took your sons and daughters whom you bore to me and sacrificed them as food to the idols. Was your prostitution not enough? You slaughtered my children and sacrificed them to the idols. In all your detestable practices and your prostitution you did not remember the days of your youth, when you were naked and bare, kicking about in your blood. . . . Because you did not remember the days of your youth but enraged me with all these things, I will surely bring down on your head what you have done, declares the Sovereign LORD. Did you not add lewdness to all your other detestable practices?'" (Ezekiel 16:20-22,43).

By our sin and rebellion, we have broken the marriage covenant God made with us. What are the just consequences of breaking the covenant? God should wash his hands of us and leave us lying in our own filth! But what does He do? Ezekiel continues:

> "'Yet I will remember the covenant I made with you in the days of your youth, and I will establish an everlasting covenant with you. Then you will remember your ways and be ashamed when you receive your sisters, both those who are older than you and those who are younger. I will give them to you as daughters, but not on the basis of my covenant with you. So I will establish my covenant with you, and you will know that I am the LORD'" (Ezekiel 16:60-62).

God says He will remember His marriage covenant with us *even though we have broken that covenant*. The Lord, speaking through Ezekiel, goes on:

> "'Then, when I make atonement for you for all you have done, you will remember and be ashamed and never again open your mouth because of your humiliation,' declares the Sovereign LORD."(Ezekiel 16:63).

God makes atonement for us through the blood of Jesus Christ. This is the Gospel of the new covenant, foretold by the prophet Ezekiel, centuries before Christ was born. God tells us, "I chose you. My forgiveness covers you. I provide for you. I make atonement for your sin and your rebellion."

Throughout the Old Testament, we see symbolic pictures of God's relationship with His wayward people. There was Tamar, who disguised herself as a prostitute and fooled her father-in-law Judah into committing sin with her (Genesis 38). There was Rahab, the prostitute of Jericho—yet God used her to aid Israel in its conquest of the Promised Land (Joshua 2). Ruth was a woman from Moab, an enemy nation of Israel; at the urging of Naomi, the mother of Ruth's late husband, Ruth seduced Boaz on the threshing room floor so that he would marry her (Ruth 3). Bathsheba, the wife of Uriah, was seduced and committed adultery with King David (2 Samuel 11).

Tamar, Rahab, Ruth, and Bathsheba are all women with sinful pasts—yet they are all listed in the genealogy of the Lord Jesus (Matthew 1). These sinners received grace and mercy from God, and they took their place in the kingly line of Christ. The good news of the Gospel is depicted throughout these Old Testament stories.

Paul sums up this good news: "But God demonstrates his own love for us in this: While we were still sinners, Christ died for us" (Romans 5:8). And the apostle Peter puts it this way: "He himself bore our sins in his body on the cross, so that we might die to sins and live for righteousness; 'by his wounds you have been healed'" (1 Peter 2:24).

You might ask, "Why would someone have to die for me? Why do I need to be healed?" It's because, as Paul tells us, we are all unrighteous and lost in sin:

> As it is written:
> "There is no one righteous, not even one;
> there is no one who understands;
> there is no one who seeks God.
> All have turned away,
> they have together become worthless;
> there is no one who does good,
> not even one" (Romans 3:10-12).

We have all fallen short of the perfect glory of God's righteous character. We can never measure up to His standard of righteousness. The good news of the Gospel is that God Himself has provided a means of righteousness that is not based on our performance. It's available to us through simple trusting faith in God through Jesus Christ.

That's the Gospel—and it changes everything.

Have you responded to the Gospel—the good news that you're accepted by God, based on the death and resurrection of His Son, Jesus? There's liberation in that good news. It frees us to obey God out of grateful delight—not fear, not a sense of duty. That simple Gospel message has changed my life. I've seen it change the lives of hundreds of people, as I've journeyed with Jesus and shared that good news along the way.

The Gospel can change your life. And your marriage, too.

QUESTIONS FOR STUDY OR GROUP DISCUSSION

11 | Win the Crowd!

1. The author lists a number of ways that covenant marriage is a symbolic picture of Christ and His church. How does this interpretation of the meaning and significance of marriage change the way you think about *your* marriage? Explain your answer.

2. Explain in your own words the meaning of the Gospel.

   - How does the Christian gospel differ from every other religion on earth?

   - Has your understanding of the Gospel changed after reading this chapter? If so, how has it changed?

3. What do you think the author means when he writes, "The Gospel is everything."

   - Is the Gospel "everything" to you? Why or why not?

4. Ezekiel 16 describes a bride who received many precious gifts and blessings from her bridegroom—then she became prideful and engaged

in idolatry and prostitution. Yet the bridegroom remembered the covenant he had made with her and he took her back and forgave her. Do you identify with this bride? Why or why not?

5. Do you feel confident that your sins are forgiven and you are accepted by God? Why or why not?

12
WHO IS YOUR CROWD?

I like to take my boys out to the drug store for ice cream cones. The ice cream at the drug store is good and it's inexpensive, and we have a great outing while giving their mom a little reprieve.

One time, we were at the ice cream counter and I said, "Okay, guys, it's one scoop, so choose wisely." So Trevor chose chocolate chip and Owen and Cole each got a scoop of rainbow sherbet. Then they took off down the aisle to look at the toys.

After they left, I ordered *my* ice cream—two scoops, of course, because I'm the dad. Then I sauntered down the aisle with my two scoops and they looked up at me—and they looked at their own cones. "Dad," said Trevor, "you told us only *one* scoop!"

Suddenly, that ice cream was sticking in my throat. "Yeah, I said that, but there's a difference between big boys and little boys, and—"

"I'm a big boy," Trevor declared.

"Well, yeah, for a little boy, you're *kind of* a big boy. But I'm a *big* boy, see?"

Well, they *do* see. They notice everything—even grownup hypocrisy.

Our kids have a built-in hypocrisy detector, and a keen eye for unfairness. They won't let us get away with a thing!

Your kids are part of your crowd—some of the closest, most profoundly influenced members of your crowd. They are watching you at close range. They can tell if you are going to church as a family to worship the Lord—or if you are dropping your kids off at Sunday school because it's free child-care. They can tell if prayer and Bible study are an integral part of your family life—or an add-on you use to camouflage the spiritual emptiness of your life.

They can tell if you and your spouse are dealing with marital conflicts by biblical principles—or by your own selfish, stubborn will.

If you want to win your crowd to Christ, a superficial façade of "churchianity" won't do. You've got to start living the Gospel—for real, for keeps, and out loud—if you are going to win the crowd. It's time to stop playing church and start getting real with God. It's time to go to Him in all humility and say, "Lord, wash me, forgive me, change me, work in me, and renew me so that I can win the crowd for you—beginning at home, beginning with my own spouse and kids."

God is *for* you

God loves us with a gracious, forgiving, covenant love. And we are to love one another with this same covenant love. Above all, we are to demonstrate this kind of love in our marriage relationships, so that the world will see God's love in action. When the people around us see Christlike love at work in the real-world circumstances of daily living, they will be attracted to the Gospel. They will want to experience this love themselves.

That's why we often hear the famous Love Chapter, 1 Corinthians 13, read at weddings. It describes for us the covenant love God showed us when He sent His Son to die for us. That special kind of love, God's covenant love, is patient and kind, it doesn't envy or boast, it's never proud or self-seeking, it doesn't dishonor others or become easily angered, and it forgets the scoreboard. Covenant love takes no pleasure in evil but always finds joy in the truth. It protects, trusts, hopes, perseveres—and it never fails.

That's not just love—that's good news! That's the Gospel that God wants us to share with the whole world. But first, he wants us to receive this love and share it with one another in our marriage relationships.

In Luke 15, Jesus tells a series of stories to show us what God's love for us is like, what the Gospel is all about. He tells about a shepherd with a hundred sheep. When the shepherd loses one of his flock, he goes off in search of that wayward sheep. The message of the Gospel is that, no matter how far you may have strayed from Him, God is after you, God is pursuing you—not to harm or hurt you, but to rescue you. He wants to carry you across his shoulders to the place of safety, to the protective enclosure of His love. When the shepherd returns home with his lost sheep, he's so happy he throws a party.

Jesus also tells us that God's love for us is like a woman who has ten coins, and she loses one. So she goes all around the house, turning on every light, overturning every sofa cushion, looking under the bed, until at last she finds that lost coin. And when she finally has that coin in her hands, she is so excited she throws a party.

These stories precede the best-loved of all of the parables of Jesus, the story of the prodigal son and the loving father. It's the story of a self-centered young man who demands his half of his inheritance while his father is still living, then goes off and squanders it all on wine and prostitutes.

After wasting all his money, losing his friends, and sinking to the depths of despair and degradation, he decides to return home and beg his father to take him in as a mere servant. The young man has his whole speech planned out: "Father, I have sinned against heaven and against you. I am no longer worthy to be called your son; make me like one of your hired servants."

So the boy heads home and, Jesus says, "while he was still a long way off, his father saw him." While he was still a long way off! Isn't that amazing? The father must have gone out to watch for his son every day, hoping he would return home—and then, one day, the loving father saw his wayward son out in the distance, "while he was still a long way off."

The father ran to the son and hugged him and kissed him, and while the son was trying to deliver his little speech, the father called his servants and said, "Quick! Bring the best robe and put it on him. Put a ring on his finger and sandals on his feet. Bring the fattened calf and kill it. Let's have a feast and celebrate! For my son was dead and is alive again; he was lost and is found."

This story in Luke 15 parallels the story in Ezekiel 16. It's a parallel of *your* story and *my* story. *We* have squandered the gifts God has given us. *We* are wayward and our hearts are unfaithful and far from him. The Lord is pursuing *us*—and while we are far off, if we just take one step toward Him, He comes running to us, just as the loving father ran to his prodigal son.

We want to come groveling before God, offering Him our religion, our works. We want to earn our way back to Him, to become His servants—but He says, "Oh, no, no, no! Don't say another word! Put this ring on, put this robe on! Let's kill the fatted calf and have a celebration! You don't have to earn your way back to Me! My son, my daughter, who was lost is now found!"

The book of Revelation tells us that God says to us, "I am making everything new!" (Revelation 21:5). That's the good news of the Gospel: "I have chosen you, I have redeemed you, I am reconciling you to myself, and I am transforming your life and making everything new."

Do you need a new and revitalized marriage relationship? He can make it new. Do you need a new relationship with your children? He can make it new. Do you need to press the "reset" button with an important friendship or family relationship in your life? He can make it new. Do you need the strength to let go of a bad habit? He can give it to you. The Gospel is the good news of transformation and newness of life. "Therefore," wrote Paul, "if anyone is in Christ, the new creation has come: The old has gone, the new is here!" (2 Corinthians 5:17).

The Gospel is God saying to us, "I love you. I hear you. I hold you. I mold you. I call you. I draw you. I see you. I seek you. I test you. I bless you. I prune you. I place you. I face you. I forgive you. I cherish you. I delight in you. I nourish you. I love you!"

That's why the apostle Paul can say—and why you and I can say along with him—"For I am not ashamed of the gospel, because it is the power of God that brings salvation to everyone who believes" (Romans 1:16a).

And Paul also wrote, "What, then, shall we say in response to these things? If God is for us, who can be against us? He who did not spare his own Son, but gave him up for us all—how will he not also, along with him, graciously give us all things?" (Romans 8:31-32). Do you believe that? Do you know that God is *for* you? If God would give His own Son for you, what blessing will He not give you?

God is on your side. He is on your marriage partner's side. He is *for* your marriage. He is *for* your family. That is the good news of the Gospel, and it is good news for your marriage relationship. This amazing message of God's love and grace for a broken humanity is what covenant marriage is all about. When God is at the center of your marriage relationship, when you live out the good news of the Gospel through your love for each other, your marriage fulfills its deepest, highest purpose.

Your marriage becomes a witness for Jesus Christ, attracting the people around you—family members, friends, neighbors, co-workers—to the good news of the Gospel. All of the people you come in contact with are your crowd. They are the people you, as a Christian, are called to reach with the Gospel of Jesus Christ.

There are people in our crowd that we easily overlook. Why? Because they are so close to us.

The first member of your crowd

We sometimes forget that our crowd begins with those closest to us. First and foremost, your crowd begins with your marriage partner—your husband or wife. Your crowd begins with the one you see across the breakfast table, the one you share a bed with, the one you make love to, the one you clash with.

In our culture, we often treat marriage as a box we check off on our way to other things, other places, other goals. But the Lord Jesus says, "No—don't treat marriage as an add-on or a compartment of your life. Enter into marriage as a sacred covenant, just as I entered into a covenant with the church. I'm married to the church and I gave My life to the church. I spilled my blood to serve the church. Now I'm working through the church to reach and win the crowd. I want you to work through your marriage to win the crowd as well."

Your spouse is not to be a "trophy wife" or "trophy husband," a prize you collect in you quest for your real goals of status, wealth, and prestige. Your spouse is not someone you take for granted, someone to whom you say, "We're married now, so you have to accept me. I don't have to behave like a Christian around you." Your *number one* crowd is your marriage partner! If you can't live out the Gospel with your wife or husband, then you have nothing to offer the rest of the world.

Our Christianity is not a costume we put on when we walk out the front door to greet the world. We need to practice Christlike love, grace, forgiveness, servanthood, integrity, and humility at home *first*, behind closed doors—then we will have something real to share with the world. If our Christianity is just an act for public consumption, then our Gospel is phony and we are nothing but hypocrites.

So let's get real with our number one crowd—with our spouse. Let's practice authentic Christianity in the home, twenty-four/seven. Let's throw away the scoreboard. Husband, love your wife. Wife, respect your husband.

Are you married to a non-believer, someone who doesn't believe the Gospel and follow Christ? Then remember that your spouse is your number one crowd. God's Word to us is that Christians with unbelieving spouses should consistently live out the love and grace of the Gospel "so that, if any of them do not believe the word, they may be won over without words . . . when they see the purity and reverence of your lives" (see 1 Peter 3:1-2).

When your husband or wife sees that you exhibit Christlikeness in everything you do—even in times of conflict—your spouse will see that the Gospel of Jesus Christ is not just a set of platitudes or Sunday school stories. It's the grace and truth that restores broken relationships, that provides God's strength in our weakness, that enables us to continue to love in unlovely situations. At some point, the reality of the Gospel will click, it will make sense—

And your unbelieving spouse will be won over to Christ. Your steadfast, unconditional, unselfish love will be a more powerful witness than any sermon or hymn. The Christ in you will be so attractive and so irresistible that your spouse will want to have what you have and know the One you know.

Jesus *loves* your crowd

Your kids are in the next closest circle of your crowd.

Imagine taking your kids to Marine World and you all sit in the rows closest to the killer whale show—the Splash Zone. If your kids are in the Splash Zone, they're going to get wet. When the killer whale leaps out of the water and comes down with a huge splash, you can't tell your kids, "Don't worry, guys, you're really not wet," because they will be drenched to the skin.

In the same way, your kids are in the Splash Zone of your marriage. If there's a problem or a crisis in your marriage, your kids will have front-row seats—and they will get splashed. They see us when we fight, when we lie, when we shift the blame, when we blow it, when we fall short. They have front-row seats to our displays of pettiness, bad temper, selfishness, dishonesty, and other character flaws. Kids are no fools. They know what's real—and they can spot a fake. So we'd better live the Gospel out loud for this crowd, our kids.

Our children may not get what we say, but they get what we do. Faith, values, and attitudes are more caught than taught. Our children watch us even when we think no one is looking—and they put more stock in what they see than what we say.

So while your spouse is the first member of your crowd, your kids are the second circle of your crowd, and the people in your community are the third circle of your crowd. Your community consists of your extended family, your friends, your fellow workers, your colleagues, your fellow students at school, your neighbors, the parents and kids in the youth soccer or baseball league, and all the other people you come in contact with during an average day.

And here's the important thing to remember: Jesus *loves* your crowd. He is 100 percent *for* your crowd! Jesus came to seek and to save your crowd! That's what Jesus Himself said in Luke 19:10—"For the Son of Man came to seek and to save the lost."

As Christians, we tend to think, "It's all about us." We come to church, and we're surrounded by Christians. We love the church. It's the hope of the world. And that's great, we *should* love the church.

But we need to remember that, back when God chose Israel, the people of Israel became prideful and thought, "It's all about us." That's why God said to Israel through the prophet Jeremiah, "I will ruin the pride of Judah and the great pride of Jerusalem." In other words, God had to tell Israel, "You've got it wrong. I didn't choose you because you were better people than those other nations. I chose you, Israel, because I wanted to use you to reach the world. I wanted to bring forth from among your people a Savior—my Son, Jesus. I love you, Israel, but not *just* you. So don't be prideful."

God loves you and blesses you, but not *just* you. He wants to work through you and your marriage. He wants to work through your relationship with your kids. He wants to work through your relationships in your community, your circle of friends, your circle of influence. He wants to win your crowd as you live out the Gospel of Jesus Christ.

Jesus always ministered to the crowd. He stopped and took time for the crowd and He built relationships with the crowd. He was interruptible for the crowd. He shared His life with the crowd.

Now He wants to live that same life through you. He wants to love the crowd and minister to the crowd through your daily life. So each day, as you go to work, or walk in your neighborhood, or enter your classroom, or wait in line at the grocery store—stop and look around at the faces of your crowd. Pray for those people, then ask God to help you live out the Gospel for those people to see and hear. Dedicate your marriage to living the Gospel out loud before your crowd.

It's significant that Ephesians 5, Paul's teaching on marriage, comes in the midst of a section of Ephesians where Paul says, in effect, "I'm going to teach you how to live Christ-honoring lives, so that you will attract unbelievers to the Gospel." In Ephesians 4, Paul taught the Christians in Ephesus to be unified and spiritually mature, to live humbly together, to be truthful and honest, to treat each other with kindness, compassion, and forgiveness. In the first half of Ephesians 5, he taught that Christians should "live as children of light" and "be filled with the Spirit."

The purpose of all these teachings about Christian living is to teach us to live as light in a dark world. Our lives are to be living demonstrations of the reality of the Gospel. And in the midst of this teaching on how to live as light, Paul instructs us on how to live out the Gospel through our marriage relationships.

After his instruction on marriage, Paul goes on in Ephesians 6 to teach about parent-child relationships and employer-employee relationships. And he concludes his discussion with his famous passage on "the full armor of God," our spiritual protection in the age-old struggle against the enemy of our souls. He wants us to be fully protected as he sends us out into the world to win the crowd.

In the midst of Paul's instruction about living out the Gospel and preaching the Gospel, he writes this marvelous passage in Ephesians 5—a set of instructions designed to transform our marriages into living billboards for the Christian Gospel. God wants to awaken a desire in the people around us—a desire to know Jesus, a desire to experience His love and power in their own marriage relationships. The Lord wants to bless your marriage and work through your marriage to win the crowd.

How is the Gospel of Jesus Christ going to spread across our nation and infect our culture? It won't happen because we pass a law or elect a certain leader. There is only one way it will happen: Christians must live out the Gospel in their everyday lives. It begins with you, it begins with me, and it begins at home, in the covenant relationship between a godly man and a godly woman—living the Gospel out loud.

QUESTIONS FOR STUDY OR GROUP DISCUSSION

12 | Who is Your Crowd?

1. How does God's love for you affect the way you love others?

   - Recall a time when you were hurt or angered, and it was hard to forgive. Does the fact that God has forgiven your worst sins help you to forgive the person who hurt you? Why or why not?

2. Read the story of the prodigal son and his loving father in Luke 15:11-32. Who is the character in that story you most identify with? Explain your answer.

3. Do you believe God is for you or against you? Explain your answer.

   - How does your answer to this question affect the way you view your marriage relationship?

4. Who are the most important people in your crowd? Name at least one person who doesn't live under your own roof.

- What are some specific steps you can take this week to live the Gospel out loud toward each of those people?

5. In the past few weeks, has anyone been in your "Splash Zone"? In other words, at some time in the past few weeks, did you behave as a poor example of what a Christian is supposed to be?

- What specific action steps could you take to right the wrong you did? How might that action be a way of "living the Gospel out loud"?

13
LIVE OUT LOUD!

Over the years, I've learned that if I prepare to speak on a certain subject then I can bet I'm going to be tested on it in my everyday life. That's exactly what happened to me as I was about to give the final talk in a three-week series on marriage at the Neighborhood Church.

The first two talks had gone well, and I was feeling pretty good. But on the Saturday before the final talk, I had one of *those* days—the kind of day where everything goes wrong. I looked out the front window and saw that I had mowed the lawns too short the previous day—the grass looked yellow and patchy, not green and healthy-looking. It was like a bad haircut—I'd have to wait for it to grow back.

We took the kids out to breakfast at the waffle place, but the French toast was gooey and sickly-sweet, and I didn't feel good after breakfast. I stopped at Peet's for a cup of coffee—but the brew was too weak. We went to get some school supplies for my son Trevor, and the prices were just outrageous.

Our three boys were just a handful that morning. Trevor wouldn't stop teasing his two brothers and making them yell. Owen, our four-year-old, was whiny. Cole, our two-year-old, was especially poopy. I was short-tempered with my boys, and I was unpleasant company for Bridget.

Obviously, none of these problems compares with a *real* trial like having cancer or losing your home. It was just one of those days when everything gets under your skin and nothing seems to go right. I was asking, "Lord, how do I turn this thing around? I've got a sour outlook right now. I've got a bad attitude as a husband, a father, and frankly, as a pastor."

Later, I went to my study and opened up God's Word to prepare for Sunday's message. Glancing over my notes, I remembered what I was planning to speak about the next morning: God's plan to use covenant marriage as an expression of His grace and love to humanity.

Had I been living out God's grace and love throughout that day? Was it an expression of God's grace and love for me to let my buzz-cut lawns, the too-sweet breakfast, the weak coffee, the overpriced school supplies, or my teasy, whiny, poopy boys to upset my entire attitude? What kind of Christian example was I setting? What kind of Christian witness was I being?

I felt God, in His gentleness and graciousness, whispering to me and saying, "Silly, proud pastor. You thought I would send you out to teach others about my Gospel. But first I had to teach you how much *you* need My grace and My love. I had to show you how far you've fallen from living out the message I gave you to share."

There's more to this story, and I'll share that in a moment. For now, let me just confess that I need God's grace and love. You need His grace and love, too. In Ephesians 5, we find out how we can not only receive God's grace and love for our own lives, but we learn how to transform our marriages into living, vibrant expressions of God's grace and love to a hurting world.

What is the Gospel? The Gospel is everything. It's our reason for living, our motivation for loving. It's the all-encompassing, all-empowering message of light and hope for a dark and despairing world.

Who is our crowd? Our crowd is our spouse, our kids, and our community.

Now the question is: How do we do win the crowd? In the closing pages of this book, we're going to learn how to win the crowd by living the Gospel out loud.

1. Winning the crowd through repentance and forgiveness

What are the key themes of the Gospel message?

The essence of the Gospel is very simple: You and I are sinners, and we have fallen short of God's standard of perfect righteousness. But God made it possible for us to be saved from the punishment we deserve by giving His

Son Jesus to die in our place. If we confess our sin and place our trust in Jesus, He will forgive us and come into our lives as Lord and Savior—and we will live with Him, now and forever.

As you read through the New Testament, you see this Gospel message expressed again and again in two words: repentance and forgiveness. John the Baptist preached "a baptism of repentance for the forgiveness of sins" (Luke 3:3). Jesus sent His disciples to preach the message of "repentance for the forgiveness of sins" (Luke 24:47). And the apostle Paul tells us that, in Christ, "we have redemption, the forgiveness of sins" (Colossians 1:14). And the apostle John tells us, "If we confess our sins, he [God] is faithful and just and will forgive us our sins and purify us from all unrighteousness" (1 John 1:9).

If we want to demonstrate the reality of the Gospel to our crowd, we have to practice *repentance and forgiveness* in our marriage relationships. That's the heart of the Gospel. That's the message of Christ's love for the Church.

You may think, "Okay, so the Gospel is all about repentance and forgiveness. No problem. If my spouse comes to me in repentance, then I will forgive."

If that's what you think, you've missed the whole point of the Gospel! Christ died for us while we were in rebellion against God. He initiated forgiveness toward us while we were still sinners, while we were wandering far from Him. He didn't wait for us to repent—He initiated, He forgave, He sacrificed Himself for us. The apostle Paul says that God, who reconciled us to Himself, has given us "the ministry of reconciliation" and He has also "committed to us the message of reconciliation" (see 2 Corinthians 5:18-19). So in our relationships at home, with our marriage partner and our kids, in our community, in our crowd, we are Christ's ambassadors living out the Gospel message of reconciliation.

I have to confess that I am not by nature a quick reconciler. I don't always initiate reconciliation like I should. Returning to the story of my bad-attitude

Saturday—the day my lawns were too short and so on and so forth—I was a very poor initiator of reconciliation. Later that afternoon, when the boys were down for their naps and the house was quiet and I was doing a bit of reading, Bridget came to me and said, "Are you all right?"

Notice who initiated? Not me—Bridget! That was a failure on my part. And, I'm sad to say, it gets worse.

"No," I said, "I'm not all right. I don't know why my attitude is so bad, but I'm sorry." Now, that would have been an excellent place to stop. A simple apology, no excuses, end of story. But I didn't stop there.

"I think the reason I acted that way," I continued, "was that I was tired and the lawns were too short and the French toast was too sweet—" And I gave qualifier after qualifier—and the longer I talked, the more I compromised my apology. A compromised apology is *not* an apology. It's not reconciliation. It's just a string of excuses.

Husband, this message is especially for you: There's a difference between *penitence*—being sorry for your sins—and *repentance*—an uncompromised apology with a commitment to change. I was penitent—but I was not repentant. I was sorry, but I was making excuses for myself.

The next morning, Sunday morning, I finally did what I should have done on Saturday. I called Bridget and my boys together and circled them around me. (Fact is, I thought I'd better make a *real* apology, *real* repentance, and a *real* reconciliation before I got up in front of the church to preach and was struck by lightning!) I literally got down on my knees so I could look my three boys in the eye, and I said, "Boys, you know that Daddy had a bad attitude yesterday. I didn't behave the way I should have. And I just want you to know that I'm sorry. Will you forgive me?"

The boys said, "Yeah, Daddy, we love you."

I looked at Bridget. "And will you forgive me, too?"

Bridget said, "Of course, honey."

I'm a little slow—but I'm learning. We need to practice repentance and forgiveness in our marriage relationship, in our parent-child relationships, and with our friends and co-workers and family members, over and over and over again.

The longer I've been married and the more marital and pre-marital counseling I've done, the more I am convinced that we need to spend more time understanding repentance and forgiveness. When I counsel couples who are about to get married, they usually tell me what a wonderful relationship they have. I say, "Okay, I know you're in love, everything is great, the wedding is going to be awesome—but what are you going to do when you fight?"

Because there will be fights in that marriage, no matter how "wonderful" the relationship may be. He's a sinner. She's a sinner. And when you put two sinners together under one roof, you can count on it—there will be a spontaneous combustion of sin! There will be conflicts to be resolved, hurts to be healed, and wrongs to be repented of and forgiven. That's the only way to live the Gospel out loud in a marriage—and you have to do it again and again. And just when you're sick of repenting and forgiving, you'll have to repent and forgive all over again.

2. To win your crowd, revel in your role

What is the role of a Christian wife, a Christian husband? Paul sums up these roles in Ephesians 5. He writes, "Wives, submit yourselves to your own husbands as you do to the Lord" (Ephesians 5:22). And he writes, "Husbands, love your wives, just as Christ loved the church and gave himself up for her" (Ephesians 5:25).

This is the call of God upon our lives. These are the roles God has designed for us. So revel in the role God has given you. Don't resist it—relish it. Don't rebel against it, revel in it! Live it to the hilt. Be the wife or husband God designed you to be.

If you are a wife, you might ask, "How do I revel in this role?" Answer: Enjoy this role. Pour yourself into the role of wife and mother. Make the most of every minute you get to spend with your husband and children. This doesn't mean you can't work outside the home, as long as you are still able to fulfill your primary role. My wife Bridget must be Wonder Woman, because she is an incredible mom, an incredible wife, yet she also works outside the home one day a week (that's the day I take over some of her duties with the house and the boys).

Or, if you are a husband, you might ask, "How do I revel in my role?" Answer: Rise up and be a godly man, a godly husband, a godly father. Pour yourself into that role and make the most of it. Train yourself to think about your wife and children, and to ask yourself, "What will my wife need most from me when I'm home? What will my kids need from me? How can I actively love my family as Christ loved the church and gave Himself for it?"

When you're driving home after work, and you're dead tired, and you're tapped out physically and emotionally, you'll be tempted to think, "I'm glad this day is over. I can't wait to get home, kick back, and enjoy the evening without any responsibilities." As a husband and father, you need to realize that when you leave the office, your *real* day is just beginning.

Now you get to go home and revel in your role of being a husband and father. That commute time is a great transition time—a few minutes when you get to think about your role, pray for your wife and kids, pray for the wisdom and strength to be all that they need you to be. Pray for the sensitivity that comes from the Holy Spirit—the ability to be sensitive to the emotional and spiritual needs of your family.

During my twenty-minute drive home from the church office, I set aside the problems of the office, and I focus and prepare myself to connecting with my kids and focus on their needs. Bridget and I have a name for that time when I, in my role as father, engage with my kids in a special way. We call it The Three B's—Bath, Books, and Bedtime. That's a valuable chunk of time for my kids—and for me. I find that I can't just let it happen. I have to charge myself up before I walk through the door.

Once I arrive home, I'll have three, maybe four hours with my kids before it's their bedtime. That means I have three or four hours to be a loving, molding, guiding, disciplining, repenting, forgiving, teaching, role-modeling dad to my kids. I want to give it all I've got! I want to revel in that role and relish that role—because it goes by all too quickly. My boys are growing up right before my eyes. So I thank God for these few golden hours each night. I don't want to waste a moment of that precious time I get to share with my kids.

The time you spend with your children is priceless teaching time. And I'm not just talking about the lessons and values you teach your kids—I'm talking about the lessons they'll teach you! You walk into the house, and your kids greet you and love you unconditionally. You might be having a bad day. You might even be kind of bad at being a dad that day—but your kids will love you anyway. Learn from their unconditional love—and then try to show that same unconditional love to others around you.

Just before Trevor, our oldest, started kindergarten, Bridget and I visited his classroom for Back to School night. We sat in those tiny little kindergarten chairs and looked around the room—then we looked at each other and could read each other's thoughts: *Our baby boy starts kindergarten tomorrow! He'll be going away to school every day!* I know, it's not like he's going away to college, but it's still a big milestone in his life—and an emotional time for us.

There are many milestones in a child's life. Savor them. Relish them. Don't you dare miss even one. There'll be other times for watching that game on TV or going out with the guys, but when your kids are grown and you can never get those times back, I hope you'll have memories of the time you spent with your kids, being their dad, loving them and receiving their love in return.

Christian husband, Christian father, Christian wife, Christian mother—revel in your role.

3. To win the crowd, center your home around God

Our job as Christian wives and husbands, moms and dads, is not just to provide food, shelter, and clothing for our kids. Our most important job is to raise them in a God-centered home. Decades from now, if my kids are asked, "What was it like growing up in the Scott household?," I want them to say, "I grew up in a house where God was always at the center." I want my kids to know that God is beautiful, majestic, powerful, and unimaginably awesome. I want them to know that every good thing—from the house we live in to the food we eat, from the stars in the night sky to the sunshine on our faces, from the backyard swing set to the beauty of the Grand Canyon—is a gift from God.

In my role as a Christian husband and father, I'm continually reminded of the words of the Psalmist:

> My people, hear my teaching;
>   listen to the words of my mouth.
> I will open my mouth with a parable;
>   I will utter hidden things, things from of old—
> things we have heard and known,
>   things our ancestors have told us.
> We will not hide them from their descendants;
>   we will tell the next generation
> the praiseworthy deeds of the LORD,
>   his power, and the wonders he has done (Psalm 78:1-4).

This is the God we serve, the God who loves us, the God who provides for us. Every day, let's find new ways to reveal to our children the wonders and mercies of our God. Let's make sure our kids know Him—not as a cosmic killjoy, but as a loving Heavenly Father; not as a remote and forbidding Judge in the sky, but as the One whom Jesus addressed in prayer as "Abba!"—the Aramaic word for "Papa!" or "Daddy!" Jesus saw God the Father as a loving Daddy, and that is how we want our kids to see Him. We don't have to fear God or hide our struggles from Him. We can climb into His lap, throw our arms around His neck, and share all our hurts and struggles with Him.

Christian husband, Christian father, center your home around God.

4. To win the crowd, walk through open doors

Does the word "evangelism" make you uneasy? Do you feel intimidated by the idea of "winning the crowd," of being a "witness" for Christ? Don't feel pressured. You don't have to win people to Christ. In fact, you can't do it. God Himself does the work of winning people to Himself. All you and I have to do is walk through open doors.

What do I mean by that? Let me give you an example from my own experience. When Bridget and I moved into our neighborhood a few years ago, a neighbor couple, George and Robin, introduced themselves and helped us move in. That day, Bridget and I began praying for George and Robin. "Lord," we said, "give us a chance to walk through doors that You open so that we can influence our neighborhood for You, beginning with George and Robin."

An open door is any time a neighbor says, "Hey, do you want to come over and hang out?" And you say, "Sure, I'll walk through that door." Or, "Hey, would you like to come over and watch *American Idol* with us?" And you say, "Sure, I'll walk through that door."

Neighbors open doors for neighbors all the time. You invite your neighbors to a backyard barbecue. They invite you out to a movie. You and your neighbors hold a two-family yard sale together. You invite them to a play or a Christmas musical at your church. The doors keep opening, and you just walk through.

Then, one day, God's grace breaks through and there's a moment when your neighbor says, "Wait, you have something I want. Please tell me more about God."

That's what happened with George and Robin. God did the work, and Bridget and I just walked through the doors He opened. Today, George and Robin are living for Christ, and growing in their relationship with Him. A couple years ago, I started a small group Bible study with George and few other men from our community. And I keep seeing amazing growth in George as he is living the Gospel out loud.

One day, I saw George walking his dog in the neighborhood, and he greeted me with a huge smile. "Hey, Tyler," he said, "I've got big news for you. I got so upset at work the other day! Someone stole a client from me!"

Well, that stumped me. "You lost a client? Why are you smiling?"

"Because we just studied James 1 in our Bible study. I remembered what James wrote, 'Consider it pure joy, my brothers and sisters, whenever you face trials of many kinds, because you know that the testing of your faith produces perseverance.' Tyler, I'm learning to 'consider it pure joy.'"

I thought, *Wow! God has really gotten hold of George's heart!* And I knew it was not because I'm a good guy or a great pastor or a perfect role model. There have been plenty of times when George saw me at my worst, plenty of times when he saw me lose my temper with my kids or be less than loving toward Bridget. George lives right next door, just over the fence, so he could certainly tell that I was no super-Christian.

But God does the work, and He chooses to work through common, ordinary human clay like me. His love and grace work through us in spite of our flaws and sins. He opens the doors, and all we have to do is willingly, obediently walk through those open doors.

We all have Georges in our neighborhoods, our families, the places where we work. Who is your George? Ask God to open a door in that person's life—then watch for opportunities. When the door opens, walk right through.

God designed marriage to be a place of love, support, and protection for you and your spouse. He designed it to be a safe place where children could be born and grow physically, emotionally, and spiritually. But more than that, He designed marriage to be a picture of Christ's relationship with the church, a living depiction of the Gospel message.

What is the Gospel? The Gospel is the good news of God's grace and forgiveness for you and me, and it applies to every area of our lives! Who is your crowd? Your spouse, your kids, your community. How do you win the crowd? Not by pretending to be a plaster saint, but by practicing a lifestyle of repentance and forgiveness, relishing the role of wife and mother, husband and father, centering your home around God, and obediently walking through the doors God opens.

Open the windows!

Jesus performed His first miracle at a wedding—the wedding at Cana in John 2. He turned water into wine. It was a miracle with a message—a sign of His authority, a convincing evidence of His lordship. Through this sign, Jesus announced, in effect, "I have come with the power to transform everything; I have come to make all things new." John 2:11 tells us, "What Jesus did here in Cana of Galilee was the first of the signs through which he revealed his glory; and his disciples believed in him."

The disciples first came to faith in Christ at the wedding in Cana—a wedding that symbolized the union of Christ and His people. The Lord chose a wedding as the place where He would be revealed in power, and where faith in Him would first be recorded. God still uses marriage as a means of reaching the world with the good news of Jesus Christ. As the prophet Isaiah wrote:

> I delight greatly in the LORD;
>   my soul rejoices in my God.
> For he has clothed me with garments of salvation
>   and arrayed me in a robe of his righteousness,
> as a bridegroom adorns his head like a priest,
> and as a bride adorns herself with her jewels
> (Isaiah 61:10).

The Book of Revelation tells us that, even in heaven, the Lord's union with His people will be pictured as a wedding celebration:

> "Let us rejoice and be glad
>   and give him glory!
> For the wedding of the Lamb has come,
>   and his bride has made herself ready.
> Fine linen, bright and clean,
>   was given her to wear."
>
> (Fine linen stands for the righteous acts of God's holy people.)
>
> Then the angel said to me, "Write this: Blessed are those who are invited to the wedding supper of the Lamb!" And he added, "These are the true words of God" (Revelation 19:8-9).

As Christians, we have the privilege and the responsibility to live as light in the world, attracting the crowd around us to Jesus Christ and His good news. Imagine the joy of sitting down at the wedding supper of the Lamb along with all the people who have come to know the Lord because of your witness, because you have faithfully lived out the Gospel through your covenant marriage relationship. Imagine hearing those people say to you, "I'm here in heaven because of the way God spoke to me through your marriage."

Jesus said, "While I am in the world, I am the light of the world" (John 9:5). But He also said, "You are the light of the world.... Let your light shine before men, that they may see your good deeds and praise your Father in heaven" (see Matthew 5:14,16). When Jesus left this world, He entrusted to us the responsibility and the privilege of lighting up the world with His love. He wants to use your marriage as a way of reaching your little corner of the human race with the light of the Gospel.

So win the crowd—live the Gospel out loud! Throw open the windows of your marriage and *let your light shine.*

QUESTIONS FOR STUDY OR GROUP DISCUSSION

13 | Live Out Loud

1. When was the last time your Christian character was tested by an upsetting problem or a series of annoying circumstances. How did you respond? Did you pass or fail that test?

    - If you failed, what specific action can you take this week to transform failure into redemption?

2. Have you ever seen Christian repentance and forgiveness powerfully lived out in the lives of people you know (parents, relatives, friends, fellow Christians)? How did seeing those acts of repentance and forgiveness impact your life?

3. Have you ever given a compromised apology—an "apology" surrounded by qualifiers and excuses? Why did you feel the need to make excuses? Why didn't you simply say, "I was wrong, I'm sorry, please forgive me"?

    - Whom do you admire more—the person who gives a "compromised apology" or the person who gives a simple "I'm sorry" apology without excuses? Explain your answer.

- In your opinion, which person is a more compelling witness for the Gospel of Jesus Christ—the person who seems to live a perfect life—or the person who sometimes sins and stumbles, but is quick to confess, repent, and ask forgiveness? Explain your answer.

4. To parents: Imagine your kids five, ten, or twenty years from now. If someone asks them, "What was it like growing up in your home?"—what would they say? Would they say, "I grew up in a house where God was always at the center"?

    - Why or why not?

    - What action steps should you take today to make your home what you want it to be—and what God wants it to be?

5. When you think of your "crowd" in your neighborhood, whose faces do you see?

    - Have you prayed for those people? Are you asking God to use you to win them to Himself? Are you asking God to open doors for you to walk through to win them to Christ?

6. Have you committed your own life to Jesus Christ? If not, what is holding you back?

If you would like to ask Jesus to become your Lord and Savior, you can do so right now. You can begin by sincerely praying this prayer of commitment:

Heavenly Father,
Thank You for your love and grace in my life. I confess that I have sinned again and again—but Lord, I'm truly sorry for my sins. I repent of my sins, and I ask You to forgive me. I invite You into my life as my Lord and Savior. Please seal this decision, fill me with your Holy Spirit, and help me live the rest of my life for You.
I ask this in Jesus' name, Amen.

EPILOGUE
DO YOU NEED A MIRACLE?

On the morning of Saturday, January 15, 2011—while this book was being written—Bridget and I got our boys up early to make sandwiches and pack lunches for the homeless. In recent weeks, God had been opening their eyes to the street people we saw regularly in the community around our northern California church. The boys had been asking questions: Don't those people have a place to live? Don't they have food to eat? God has blessed our boys with compassionate hearts, so we were all going to do our part to live out the gospel by feeding the homeless.

We gathered up the food we had prepared, loaded everyone in the car, and started off toward church. Just a mile down the road, my phone buzzed, announcing an incoming text. A quick glance at my phone made my heart sink: "Call France's cell. Your dad was rushed to hospital. In critical condition. Deborah." France is Dad's wife, my step-mom. Deborah is a family friend.

I pulled the minivan over, and Bridget and I exchanged glances that said it all. I turned around to face my three boys in the back seat. "Guys," I said, "I jut found out that something has happened to Papa Terry." (That's what they call their grandpa.) "Let's all pray for him right now. . . . Lord, we don't know what happened, but please protect my dad, please watch over Papa Terry. This is not a surprise to you. This is not too big for you. You can heal anyone. You can heal any body, any heart, at any time. So we pray that, if it would be your will to heal Papa Terry, please heal him fully, for the glory of Your Name. Amen."

We turned the car around and dropped the boys at the home of some friends. Then Bridget and I rushed an hour north to the hospital in Napa where Dad had been taken. On the way, we exchanged texts and phone calls with friends and relatives, trying to piece together what had happened. Here's what we later found out:

Dad had been out for his regular morning walk with Deacon, his German shepherd. About a mile from home, he recognized a neighbor lady who was jogging toward him on the other side of the street, along the edge of a golf course. Dad raised his hand to wave a greeting—

And at that instant, he was struck by a massive heart attack.

The attack was so sudden and so massive that he fell straight back, slamming his head on the sidewalk. In addition to the heart attack, he suffered a fractured skull from the fall, with multiple concussions and traumatic brain injury (TBI). As Dad lay there, his heart stopped beating—and stopped supplying oxygen to his body and brain. Blood streamed from the back of his head.

The jogger had seen all of this, and she ran to Dad's side and quickly sized up the situation. She turned toward the street and flagged down an approaching car. The driver rolled down his window, and the lady called frantically, "Call 911!"

A few other people ran up to see if they could help—but seeing my father lying motionless on the concrete, they didn't think anything could be done for him. In fact, given the severity of his heart attack and head injury, he probably should have died right there. But God had a different plan.

Just then, a golfer drove his cart up to the tee box at the golf course. Noticing the commotion across the way, he paused for a better look—and recognized my dad's dog. "That's Deacon," he said aloud—then he recognized my dad. "My goodness, that's Terry Scott!" The golfer—a retired airline pilot—was a friend of my father's.

He leaped from the cart and sprinted toward my dad, sizing up the situation on the run. Fortunately, he had undergone extensive CPR training—and he had nerves of titanium steel. The onlookers stepped aside as he moved in and took charge. He checked my dad's pulse . . . *nothing*.

Realizing that the next few seconds meant life or death for my father, he pressed his hands over Dad's chest and began pumping his heart. Then he did mouth-to-mouth resuscitation, forcing air into Dad's lungs. At first, there was no response—then, after about half a minute, the man checked again, and found a faint pulse.

About two minutes later, the fire department and paramedics arrived and took over. They stabilized Dad's head and neck, and used the defibrillator to keep his fluttering, failing heart going. Then they put him in the ambulance and rushed him to the ER. From the moment of the heart attack throughout the attempts to revive him, he had shown no signs of consciousness.

During the hour it took Bridget and me to drive to the hospital, the ER staff put my dad through a battery of tests. Finally, they made the all-important decision to place him in a medically induced coma for twenty-four to forty-eight hours. They cooled his entire body in the hope of minimizing his brain trauma and maximizing his chances for a full recovery.

Bridget and I dashed into the hospital, full of questions and fears, but sustained by our faith in God. When we reached his hospital bed, I kissed his cold forehead, wept over him, and prayed the Scriptures (especially the Psalms) over his comatose body, begging God for a miracle. His heart was damaged, his skull was broken, blood was oozing from his ears, and his brain had suffered such a blow that the doctors were very iffy about his recovery—and even his survival.

I remember the absolute stillness of that room. The only sound was the steady beeping of the monitoring machines—beep, beep, beep. Would Dad live or die? If he lived, how might his mind and personality be affected by the brain injury? How would this event affect our family, our future?

That day took our family by storm. Days, weeks, and months passed by as Dad's life and recovery hung in the balance. And each of those days was a storm in itself.

At this point, you may be thinking, "Why is Tyler telling me this story?

What does all of this have to do with my marriage relationship?" Here's the answer:

Everyone goes through storms in life. Storms are frightening and traumatic. They seem to go on and on without letup. We go through storms when the people we love are hurt, when they come close to physical death, and we feel powerless to help them. And we go through storms when the people we love hurt us, when they have broken their promises to us, when our marriage relationship comes close to death, and we feel powerless to save it.

Just as I stood at my father's bedside, wracked with fears and questions, praying for a miracle, you may be kneeling at the side of your marriage bed, questioning God, fearing the worst, praying for a miracle in your marriage and your family right now. You are going through a storm in your marriage, and that storm is going on and on without letup. What do you do and where do you go when you feel yourself sinking and drowning as this marital storm blows through your life?

I've learned two great truths through the traumatic and stormy season I went through—and am still going through to some degree—after my father's heart attack. The first great truth I learned: *God is powerful.*

God is powerful

God still answers prayer. He can bring healing to any person, any situation, any relationship. As the psalmist wrote:

> For in the day of trouble he will keep me safe in his dwelling; he will hide me in the shelter of his tabernacle and set me high upon a rock.... I would hurry to my place of shelter, far from the tempest and storm (Psalm 27:5; 55:8).

As Dad lay in that medically induced coma, literally thousands of people in our local church family and our extended community of faith were praying for his recovery. And God answered those prayers in a mighty way. In fact, as I write these words, He is still answering those prayers.

During the first month after his heart attack and injury, Dad went from intensive care to an acute rehab center. He also went from a coma to a kind of scrambled consciousness in which he could not remember anything—or anyone. He was irritable and confused. He had memories and thoughts, but they were disorganized and random. He was physically brittle and weak. He could barely walk, and his heart almost quit on him several times.

Here was my dad, my lifelong friend, the man I had shared so many memories with—and suddenly we were like strangers. His personality was changed. His memories were gone. When we talked, I wasn't sure if he understood me, or even knew who I was.

The neurological team at the hospital gathered our family together and talked with us about Dad's future. They said that the best we could hope for was for Dad to regain the functional capacities of a twelve- to fifteen-year-old. We nodded and asked questions, and we resigned ourselves to the grim future the doctors outlined for him. And we continued praying.

Then, about a month after the accident, we all noticed a slight change in my dad. His memory and recognition were slowly coming back. A name here, a story there—and we could catch occasional glimpses of his old personality. Day by day, he made progress—but the progress was agonizingly slow.

On the doctors' advice, we moved Dad to Casa Colina in Pomona, California—a transitional living facility for people recovering from traumatic brain injuries. The day we drove Dad down and checked him in, he was still barely functional and had few memories of his life before the accident. He stayed at Casa Colina for thirty days, undergoing daily six- to eight-hour rounds of aggressive (and expensive) treatments.

But at the end of those thirty days, Dad walked out unassisted, with much of his memory and cognition intact. We were amazed to find him about 80 percent back to normal.

Dad was back. He was (mostly) himself. It was a *miracle*—and I don't throw that word around lightly. I truly believe that the power of God, working through our prayers and Dad's doctors, enabled him to leave that facility as a walking, talking, living miracle.

As I write these words, more than half a year has passed, and Dad is about 90 percent recovered. He has vastly exceeded the twelve- to fifteen-year-old mental capacity that the doctors had originally predicted. Yes, there are lingering effects of the heart attack and brain injury. His energy level and stamina are low. He seems to have aged several years in a few months.

But if you hadn't known him before, if you were meeting him for the first time, you'd never suspect that he had suffered a traumatic brain injury. He's lost about forty pounds, but with the help of a pacemaker/defibrillator, his heart is stronger and healthier than it has been in years. Dad is grateful for God's grace and healing touch. He says it wasn't God's plan for him to die that day on the sidewalk, that God had a greater purpose for healing Him. He has reprioritized his life, his marriage, and his plans for the future.

God has moved mightily in our lives—and He can move in your life as well. What are you praying for? Are you praying for your marriage? Your family? Your future? Do you need a miracle right now?

Remember, God is powerful, and He still answers prayer. He truly can bring healing to any person, any situation, any relationship.

And remember, too, that prayer is active. Prayer is anticipatory, expectant, and hopeful. And our prayers should be marked by a willingness to do whatever it takes, at whatever cost, to facilitate the means of healing God chooses to bring. That's the first great truth I learned through this experience: God is powerful.

The second great truth is this: *A healthy covenant marriage is a key to weathering the storms of life.*

A healthy covenant marriage is "storm insurance"

Wouldn't you love to be able to purchase an insurance policy to protect against the storms of life? The good news is that you can! A healthy, Christ-centered, love-enriched covenant marriage is the best form of insurance you can buy. It won't keep the storms from coming, just as Geico can't prevent you from having an auto collision. But the "storm insurance" of a healthy marriage will protect your mind, heart, and soul from being overwhelmed by the storms of life.

Storms are inevitable. But a healthy marriage can strengthen you and anchor you so that, when the storms come, you'll not only endure them and survive them, but you be able to embrace them and grow stronger through them. The storms of life actually produce spiritual fruit in our lives—the fruit of greater faith and deeper character—when we face those storms with the hope and patience that comes from God. As Paul writes:

> Not only so, but we also glory in our sufferings, because we know that suffering produces perseverance; perseverance, character; and character, hope. And hope does not put us to shame, because God's love has been poured out into our hearts through the Holy Spirit, who has been given to us (Romans 5:3-5).

God has given us the gift of marriage precisely because we cannot face these storms alone. As God said in Genesis 2:18, "It is not good for the man to be alone." And it's not good for the woman to be alone either. Solomon expressed it well in Ecclesiastes:

> Two are better than one,
>   because they have a good return for their work:
> If one falls down,
>   his friend can help him up.
> But pity the man who falls
>   and has no one to help him up!
> Also, if two lie down together, they will keep warm.

> But how can one keep warm alone?
> Though one may be overpowered,
> two can defend themselves.
> A cord of three strands is not quickly broken (Ecclesiastes 4:9-12).

What is that extra-strong cord of three strands? It is the strand of the husband, the strand of the wife, and the strand of the Lord, all joined and braided together—and that three-fold strand is very hard to break!

During the crisis of my father's heart attack, I learned that a strong, three-fold marriage cord can get us through any storm life may throw at us. Again and again, I leaned on Bridget for strength, support, insight, love, and prayer—and she was always there for me, pouring her strength into me in those times when I was emotionally spent.

Throughout those days, I was often away from home, commuting between our home and the hospital an hour away. At the same time, I was also trying to keep my commitments as a pastor, husband, and father. I often felt like I was juggling a dozen eggs at once—and fumbling most of them. Yet Bridget was always there to catch the ones I dropped, to cheer me on, to pray for me, to support me. She stood strong in the storm, and helped to keep me on a steady course.

Storms have a way of revealing the strength of a marriage. A weak and unhealthy marriage often breaks under the stress of tough times. A healthy marriage, founded on covenant love, always grows stronger in tough times. Our marriage actually flourished during the acid test of my dad's ordeal. Now that we have gone through this experience, Bridget and I have more confidence than ever of God's power and our mutual love and support.

Make no mistake: there will be stormy seasons ahead for Bridget and me—and for you and your marriage partner. Storms are inevitable in all of our lives. But the storms don't have to break us. They can make us stronger.

The storms of life also give us a golden opportunity to "live out loud" and let the light of Jesus shine in our lives, pointing the way to Him. When we go through tough times with an attitude of faith and hope, people notice. We have the opportunity to embrace our trials, an opportunity to rejoice in our sufferings, as Paul said, knowing that God will work these things together for His good in our lives.

Now, I'm not saying we should enjoy tough times. Storms are miserable. Crises are frightening. Trials are bruising to the body and soul. But tough times *build* character—and *reveal* character. After you go through a trial, you often feel a sense of exhilaration when you realize that God enabled you to outlast the storm.

And when you go through a trial with your mate, when you see how strong you are as a couple surrounded by covenant love, you *rejoice* that you were able to discover the depth and strength of your marriage. You look at each other and say, "Wow! A cord of three strands really can stand the test of tough times! Everything we've invested in making our marriage strong has paid huge dividends! The two of us plus the Lord—what an *awesome* team we make!"

Marriage is like a bank account—a "rainy day" fund. On good days, when the sun is shining, you make deposit after deposit. Even the little deposits of love, prayer, unselfishness, thoughtfulness, and kindness start to add up over time. Eventually, the "rainy days" come—a stressful, stormy season. Then it's time to make a withdrawal from the "bank account" of your covenant marriage. If you have plenty of love and faithfulness stored up in your relationship account, you're going to be just fine.

So keep making those daily deposits. Keep showing each other Christlike covenant love. Keep demonstrating mutual respect and mutual submission. Keep ignoring the scoreboard. And always keep the Lord—the third and strongest strand of that three-fold cord—always at the center of your relationship.

There may be storm clouds in the distance, but don't worry. You've got each other. You've got the Lord. Your future is very bright.

NOTES

1 | Forget the Scoreboard
1. Andy Stanley, *Staying in Love Participant's Guide: Falling in Love Is Easy, Staying in Love Requires a Plan* (Grand Rapids: Zondervan, 2010), 52, 71.

2 | The Marriage Covenant
1. My understanding of covenant marriage has been profoundly shaped and expanded by the teachings of Tim Keller, author and founding pastor of Redeemer Presbyterian Church (PCA) in New York City, New York.

6 | Naked and Unashamed
1. Randy Pausch, *The Last Lecture* (New York: Hyperion, 2008), pp. 4-6.
2. Ibid., p. 8.

8 | Hear the Call
1. Jack Bass and Walter De Vries, (Athens, GA: University of Georgia Press, 1995), 100.

11 | Win the Crowd
1. C. J. Mahaney, *Sex, Romance, and the Glory of God* (Wheaton, IL: Crossway, 2004), 24.

A WORD TO VICTIMS OF ABUSE

I've written this book for people who are in, soon to be in, or hope one day to be in a Christian marriage relationship. In these chapters we deal with the kinds of issues, problems, and dynamics that are common to all Christian marriages. Even the most healthy marriage relationship has problems that need to be understood and worked through.

But please understand that this book is not designed to help fix a marriage where there is a pattern of abuse or violence. Being married to an abusive partner is a problem that is far beyond the scope of this book.

Abusers often use various forms of destructive behavior to control people, up to and including violence. An abusive partner may use insults, name-calling, physical threats, threats of taking away the children, shaming, false accusations of infidelity, and public humiliation to control the other person. In an abusive marriage, the abuser will often try to isolate the victim and cut off contact with family members and church friends.

Some abusers use God and religious guilt to manipulate others. For example, abusive husbands often twist the Bible in order to manipulate their wives: "The Bible says you have to submit to me! If you don't do what I say, you're sinning against God!"

You should not allow yourself or your children to be controlled, threatened, or brutalized. How do you know if you are being abused?

If you have bruises or other injuries caused by your marriage partner—

If you've ever suffered embarrassment or had to call in sick or take time off from your normal schedule because of something your mate has done to you—

If you've ever lied to others to cover up for your partner's hurtful behavior—

If you worry that your kids are being harmed by your partner's behavior (for example, they've been physically harmed, they are acting out violent behavior through bullying others, or they try to protect you from your mate's abusive behavior)—

Then you probably need help that is beyond what this book offers. I strongly encourage you to contact a local support agency for help.